Best Advice for Preaching

BEST ADVICE
FOR PREACHING

Edited by
John S. McClure

FORTRESS PRESS
MINNEAPOLIS

BEST ADVICE FOR PREACHING

Book design by Joseph Bonyata.

Cover design by David Lott.

Library of Congress Cataloging-in-Publication Data

Best advice for Preaching / edited by John S. McClure.
    p.   cm.
  Includes bibliographical references.
  ISBN 0-8006-2997-3 (alk. paper)
    1. Preaching. I. McClure, John S., 1952– .
BV4211.2F47   1998
251—dc21   97–46416
                                                            CIP

Manufactured in the U.S.A.   AF 1-2997

02   01   00   99   98   1   2   3   4   5   6   7   8   9

In memory of my father
M. Scott McClure

CONTENTS

CONTRIBUTORS

JOANNA ADAMS, Senior Pastor, Trinity Presbyterian Church, Atlanta, Georgia.

RONALD J. ALLEN, Associate Professor of Preaching and New Testament, Christian Theological Seminary, Indianapolis, Indiana.

ARTHUR P. BOERS, Pastor, Bloomingdale Mennonite Church, Waterloo, Ontario.

CHARLES BUGG, former Senior Minister, Providence Baptist Church, Charlotte, North Carolina. Professor of Preaching and Worship, Baptist Theological Seminary at Richmond, Richmond, Virginia.

WALTER BURGHARDT, Senior Fellow, Woodstock Theological Center, Washington, D.C. Founder and Director, Preaching the Just Word.

JOHN R. CLAYPOOL, Rector of St. Luke's Episcopal Church, Birmingham, Alabama.

WILLIAM SLOANE COFFIN, Former Pastor, Riverside Church, New York City.

FRED CRADDOCK, Bandy Distinguished Professor of New Testament and Preaching, Emeritus, The Divinity School, Emory University, Atlanta.

MITTIES MCDONALD DE CHAMPLAIN, Associate Professor of Preaching and Communication Studies, Fuller Theological Seminary, Pasadena, California.

VIRGILIO ELIZONDO, former Rector, San Fernando Cathedral, San Antonio, Texas. Founder, Mexican-American Cultural Center, San Antonio.

LOWELL ERDAHL, Bishop Emeritus, Lutheran Church of America.

JAMES HENRY HARRIS, Pastor, Second Baptist Church, Richmond, Virginia, and Professor of Homiletics and Worship at Virginia Union University School of Theology.

APRIL LARSON, Bishop, La Crosse Area Synod, Evangelical Lutheran Church of America.

THOMAS G. LONG, Former Francis Landey Patton Professor of Preaching and Worship, Princeton Theological Seminary, Princeton, New Jersey, currently Director of Congregational Resources, Presbyterian Publishing Corporation.

CRAIG A. LOSCALZO, former Professor of Preaching, Southern Baptist Seminary, Louisville, Kentucky, currently Senior Minister, Immanuel Baptist Church, Lexington, Kentucky.

BARBARA LUNDBLAD, Pastor, Our Savior's Atonement Lutheran Church, New York City.

JOHN S. MCCLURE, Frank H. Caldwell Professor of Preaching and Worship, Louisville Presbyterian Seminary, Louisville, Kentucky.

ROBIN MEYERS, Senior Minister, Mayflower Congregational Church (UCC), Oklahoma City.

HENRY H. MITCHELL, former Professor of Preaching at the Interdenominational Theological Center in Atlanta. Currently a mentor in the Doctor of Ministry program at the United Theological Seminary in Dayton, Ohio.

DAVID H. C. READ, Minister Emeritus, Madison Avenue Presbyterian Church, New York City.

THOMAS E. RIDENHOUR, Professor of Homiletics and Academic Dean, Luther Theological Southern Seminary, Columbia, South Carolina.

BARBARA BROWN TAYLOR, Rector, Grace-Calvary Episcopal Church, Clarksville, Georgia.

LEONORA TUBBS TISDALE, Associate Professor of Preaching and Worship, Princeton Theological Seminary, Princeton, New Jersey.

THOMAS H. TROEGER, Ralph E. and Norma E. Peck Professor of Preaching and Communications, Iliff School of Theology, Denver, Colorado.

JOHN VANNORSDALL, President Emeritus, Lutheran Seminary, Philadelphia, Pennsylvania.

WILLIAM H. WILLIMON, Dean of the Chapel and Professor of Christian Ministry, Duke University, Durham, North Carolina.

J. PHILIP WOGAMAN, Senior Minister, Foundry United Methodist Church, Washington, D.C.

PREFACE

John S. McClure

Wisdom anchors an important place in any practical discipline. The wisdom literature in the Bible, for instance, dis-
closes much about the character and purposes of God and the
forms of spiritual and ethical practice that are deemed most faithful to God. In our late modern and progress-minded era, wisdom is
often misunderstood as static and irrelevant. But wisdom is
dynamic. It expands and renews itself in each generation, building
on the relevant experiences and practices of the past and present.

Best Advice for Preaching is an experiment in collaborative
homiletical wisdom. Instead of presenting the advice of one
preacher or professional homiletician, this book incorporates the
collaborative wisdom of a broad cross-section of preachers and
teachers of preaching. Twenty-seven professional homileticians
and parish or itinerant preachers have contributed: women and
men of various ages, social locations, church sizes, racial-ethnic
identities, and ecclesiastical, liturgical, and denominational
backgrounds.

The distinction between preachers and professional homileticians has always been rather arbitrary. All ten of the professional
homileticians who organized the chapters of this book do a great
deal of preaching. Most have been or are currently parish ministers.
At the same time, many of the seventeen people who constitute
"our preachers" throughout this book have taught in seminaries

and produced important—even pivotal—books on preaching. They constitute our preachers simply because they were asked to assume their personas as practicing preachers and offer the kind of clear, concise, and sometimes anecdotal advice that they would offer as a mentor or friend to a developing preacher.

Here's how the book was put together. First, in consultation with several preachers and colleagues, I formulated ten fundamental questions about the practice of preaching. I then mailed out a ten-page questionnaire to all of our preachers. At the top of each page was a question that began with the words: What is your best advice about:

- The Calling of the Preacher
- Getting a Message
- Patterns in Sermons
- Collecting Supportive Material
- Organizing Material
- Polishing the Sermon
- What to Do while Preaching
- Coordinating with the Rest of the Service
- Feedback
- Essential Resources for Preaching

After the questionnaires were returned to me, I sent the responses to the homiletician selected to write a chapter about that particular topic. The writers were given an outline and asked to write their chapters by bringing themselves and our preachers into conversation, quoting from their material as much as possible. The result is a rich and timely collection of instructions, answers to frequently asked questions, anecdotal or narrative explanations, and practical information.

Beyond the wealth of good advice in these pages, the reader should pay attention to the historical, theological, and theoretical trends that are represented in today's practical wisdom about preaching. If I were to summarize theologically what seems to have happened in North American homiletics in the past fifty years, I would have to say, after reading these chapters, that Emil Brunner and Paul Tillich seem to have had more influence on this generation than Karl Barth. Instead of focusing on the revelatory and kerygmatic characteristics of the preaching office, there is far more emphasis on the humanity of the preacher and the existential and numinous qualities of preaching.

In chapter 1, Leonora Tubbs Tisdale shows that, while our preachers are well aware of the sacred dimension of the calling to preach, they are also profoundly aware of the humanity of the preacher. She considers how this human dimension is stretched even further in this generation by the painful and sometimes political aspects of the calling to preach for those who belong to denominations and traditions that are not responsive to the calling of women to the preaching ministry. In chapter 2, Ronald Allen shows how preachers get a message to preach by using a theological method of correlation. The preacher discerns the gospel message by attending deeply to questions and concerns that arise from human existence while simultaneously exploring the Bible and theological tradition for meaningful responses. From our preachers, we can see the diverse ways that the Bible is both the source and the criterion for the preacher's message today. The Bible remains central to preaching, but it is the gospel that we preach—not the Bible itself. In chapter 3, Thomas Long takes us into the labyrinth of calendars, lectionaries, and pressing pastoral or doctrinal concerns that vie for control of the contemporary preacher's pattern of preaching. Our preachers display a remarkable flexibility in the face of these often-competing patterns. They encourage both discipline and forethought so that preaching is neither ad hoc nor tyrannized by the planning process. In chapter 4, William Willimon shows us how preachers no longer simply use illustrations to help them make their points. Instead, sermon illustrations are the result of the preacher's discernment of an analogical connection between biblical revelation and life today. In chapter 5, I explore our preachers' responses to the enormous range of options for organizing sermon materials that are available to preachers today, including deductive, inductive, narrative, and conversational models. Instead of assuming that one (propositional-deductive) shoe fits all, our preachers negotiate between their own expectations and those of their traditions and congregations.

Henry Mitchell, in chapter 6, explains how polishing a sermon is no longer a matter of achieving good standard English grammar and logical proportion. Preachers today encourage orality and concern for an experiential encounter with God. They use imagery, particularity, and the language of the heart in sermon preparation and delivery. In chapter 7 Mitties McDonald de Champlain concludes that conversation and authenticity, instead of drama and oratory, are the signposts for delivery in this generation. Natural delivery, congruence, and contextual sensitivity have replaced stateliness, persuasive effectiveness, and rhetorical power as criteria for sermon delivery. Thomas Troeger shows in chapter 8 that we have moved into a new situation in which the sermon is viewed as an integral part of worship. No longer the controlling centerpiece around which worship is thematically organized, the sermon is an act of worship in service to an entire worship event. In chapter 9, Craig Loscalzo demonstrates how remarkably open (and vulnerable) to feedback preachers have become. The variety of ways that our preachers gain, process, and use informal and formal feedback is unique to this generation of preachers. Thomas Ridenhour, in chapter 10, displays the range of resources that are at the fingertips of preachers today. Besides the usual resources of literature, biblical aids, and theology, he notes a new interest in congregational exegesis, cultural studies, psychology, spiritual formation, and continuing education among today's preachers.

More difficult to see, but present in this book, are some indicators of how current wisdom is already beginning to change. Signs show that the individualism of narrative and inductive preaching is giving way to a concern for a more communal approach to preaching. There is a sense throughout the book that the hearer of sermons is no longer the discrete individual who shares a common humanity with others seated in the pew. Instead, the hearer is a community of diverse people in search of meaningful forms of communal practice. In every chapter of this book, the concern for communal hearing and practice is a pervasive theme. This heralds many possible future directions for homiletical wisdom and practice, including pluralistic, conversational, relational, catechetical, cultural-linguistic, or praxis-oriented models. I would like to be around in fifty years to try this experiment again: to see what the next shape of homiletical wisdom will be. It certainly grows from fertile soil, as the reader will confirm after reading these pages of sound homiletical advice.

I am grateful to Cynthia Thompson at Fortress Press for providing the opportunity to pursue this difficult organizational feat. Thanks to Tonya Vickery, whose secretarial help kept things from falling into utter disarray many times. I am also grateful to colleagues Amy Plantinga Pauw, Marion Soards, Trisha Willey, Chris Elwood, Kathryn Johnson, Susan Garrett, Darrell Guder, Burton Cooper, and Joe Coalter for counsel of various sorts along the way, and to Louisville Presbyterian Seminary for sabbatical time to finish the project and get it to press. Special thanks, of course, to the contributors to this book, for their sustained excitement over this project and their patience with the process.

1

THE CALLING OF THE PREACHER

Leonora Tubbs Tisdale

Preaching is both the most rewarding and the most difficult work I do as a parish minister. After eighteen years at it, I continue to be awed by the nature of the task. In that pregnant moment in the pulpit before the first words of the sermon are spoken, I am usually filled with a heady mixture of self-consciousness and heart-skipping excitement. The latter is born of the awareness that, by the grace of God, I just might have a gift to give to the people sitting before me— the people who yearn for the experience of God and for a credible story inside of which they can live with joy and meaning. The self-consciousness comes from the all-too-evident reality that I am nothing more than an ordinary human being handling the mysteries of God. It helps me to remember that all I am required to do is to speak the truth as best I know it that day and leave the rest to the Holy Spirit.
—Joanna Adams

In these words, Joanna Adams describes not only her own experience of preaching but also the experience of countless preachers through the ages. Preaching is both weighty burden and winged joy, both grueling labor and gracious gift, both terrifying challenge and exhilarating empowerment. Preaching is born of a mysterious meeting between heaven and earth in which the divine and the

1

human, the ordinary and the extraordinary become so intertwined as to be almost indistinguishable.

So, too, the call to preach. On the one hand, that call is preeminently a divine act, a claim of God that comes from beyond and summons the believer to speak on behalf of God.

> Such a commission has some scriptural precedent in the call of Jeremiah: "Before I formed you in the womb I knew you, and before you were born I consecrated you; I appointed you a prophet to the nations" (Jeremiah 1:5). A prophet not primarily in the sense of predictor, rather, the prophet, the preacher, speaks God's word to God's people, and is, in a sense, God's mouthpiece.
>
> —Walter Burghardt

Yet preaching is also a very human act in which God uses ordinary earthen vessels as extraordinary vehicles of grace. Therein lies the humbling nature of its call.

> Neither prophet nor apostles set out with the notion of being one of God's aristocracy in responding to this call. Rather their testimony is of reluctance and a sense of unworthiness. I have always loved the way Paul described his calling to the ministry: "Unto me, who am less than the least of all the saints is this grace given, that I should preach among the Gentiles the unsearchable riches of Christ."
>
> —David H. C. Read

John Claypool honestly recounts his own mixed motives for deciding to enter a preaching ministry: a God-hunger in his own life, a desire to make the world a better place by teaching people how to live, and an urge to win his mother's blessing.

> Our calls usually involve both the best and the worst of our genuine humanity, and the miracle is that God somehow takes all of this and creates genuine good out of the less than perfect.

Preachers give testimony to a diversity of ways in which they experience God's call in their own lives. For some, the call to preach is a gradual process that develops and unfolds over a long period of time. For others, the call comes in a sudden moment of illumination. Some eagerly and willingly respond to the call, others need more convincing.

Barbara Brown Taylor recounts that her call—a twin call to preaching and celebrating the sacraments—came after she preached her first sermon.

> I delivered my first sermon on the night before Easter when I was a lay assistant at a big downtown church. Preparing the sermon turned every muscle in my body into a knot, but when I opened my mouth and the words began to come out—and when those present leaned into them, clearly interested in what came next—I decided to become a priest.

David Read says that one day in 1935 he heard a sermon in a small Baptist church in Edinburgh. He has long since forgotten the preacher's name and the sermon's text and theme. He emerged, however, knowing that he was going to prepare for the Christian ministry.

> If you had asked me as I entered that church what career I was heading for (I was just completing a degree in English literature and language), I would probably have answered: teaching, journalism, the law, diplomacy, or the stage—but most certainly not the Christian ministry. If you had asked the same question as I left that church, I would have said without hesitation: "I'm going to train for the ministry." As I discovered later, one of the marks of the Holy Spirit at work is the surprising and unexpected ways the Spirit works.

Fred Craddock tells of a pilgrimage in which, at least initially, it was important for him to distinguish between the call to ministry and the call to preach.

> Not everyone who is called to ministry is called to preach;
> there are many ministries without a pulpit. This distinction
> helped me to say "Yes" to ministry when I could not see a pul-
> pit in my future. Because of my size, weakness of voice, and
> lack of social presence, the gifts that confirm a call to preach
> were not apparent to me. Hard work, voice exercises, and the
> encouragement of others moved me toward the pulpit.

Perhaps Robin Meyers best captures both the urgency and the
persistence of call that many experience.

> A call to preach does not always come as a dramatic conver-
> sion experience (though some continue to feel vaguely guilty
> if they have never traveled the Damascan Road), but may
> come as a gradual, yet unmistakable compulsion to spread
> the word that has come to you—namely, this *is* the answer
> to the problem of human existence; this *is* the truth; this *is*
> the decisive action of a loving God. I have heard, and con-
> tinue to hear. Thus I preach as one who cannot keep silent.

The call to preach, however, is not simply a matter between the
individual and God. It is also mediated by, confirmed within, and
ratified in an ongoing way by the church of Jesus Christ.

> Each call to the preaching ministry will arise within a context
> of faith and doubt, but there will be hope for satisfaction in
> preaching if the church and I both find evidence of God at
> work in my calling.
> —John Vannorsdall

> That the church confirmed God's call to ministry was for
> me essential. Family conversations were important, but
> God seldom calls anyone in a voice loud enough for the
> whole family to hear.
> —Fred Craddock

> My calling as a preacher came from God through the church. Without the church I could have sighed in wonder, but I wouldn't have known God's name.
>
> —Barbara Lundblad

While I agree with our preachers that the call to preach should be both internally experienced and externally confirmed by the church, I am also sadly aware of the pain and frustration many women experience when the very church bodies that baptized them, nurtured them in faith, and encouraged them to obedient discipleship refuse to recognize the validity of their calls on the basis of gender alone. Faithfulness for these women often becomes a wrenching choice between obedience to the God who called them and obedience to the denomination that refuses to ordain them. In such cases it may be helpful to remember that *church* is always larger than any local manifestation of it, and that sometimes the broader wisdom of Christ's *ecclesia* is needed in assessing call. Barbara Lundblad reminds us that *Church* is sometimes spelled with a capital *C*.

In whatever way call is experienced, that God-human encounter—like Moses's startling confrontation at the burning bush, Samuel's persistent summons in the middle of the night, or Mary's unexpected visit by an angel—can be both encouraging and frightening.

> Encouraging because we can recall God's response to Jeremiah's "I don't know how to speak." Don't say that; "for you shall go to all to whom I send you, and you shall speak whatever I command you. Do not be afraid of them, for I am with you to deliver you" (Jeremiah 1:6-8). Frightening because a call from God lays heavy demands on the preacher.
>
> —Walter Burghardt

Yet for the one who is truly called, there is no running away. Walter Burghardt reminds us that there is only one appropriate response.

Enthusiastic commitment, similar to Mary's response to the angel: "Here am I, the servant of the Lord; let it be with me according to your word" (Luke 1:38).

GOALS

• Preach the gospel, always remembering that God entrusts it to us as sacred treasure.

Someone has said, "There are two kinds of preachers—those who have to say something and those who have something to say!" The call to be God's witnesses is grounded in the gift of something significant to say. That something centers in the life-giving gospel of God's grace revealed and promised in Jesus Christ. We preachers are in the business of proclaiming a message creative of the full and abundant Life Christ came to give!

—Lowell Erdahl

To be a pastor/preacher is to be called to stand on both sides of the pulpit—first as one baptized sitting in the pew with all the people with open, empty hands, waiting for the bread of life. Second, on the other side, as one who proclaims the living word of Jesus Christ that changes lives in the very act of the preaching, the proclaimer of the sacred treasure.

—April Larson

Authentic Christian preaching is an act of gift giving. When we recognize that we have been chosen by another and will be empowered by the same one, the sense of preaching as giving to another what has first been given to us graciously will become our perspective.

—John R. Claypool

• Preach in a way that helps people know how to live faithful lives in their own particular time and place in history.

> If I had to sum up what the purpose of preaching is in a sentence, I would say that it is to help people see the events in their lives and in human history from God's point of view. Preaching reshapes the human imagination so that, even in an often hopeless world, possibilities for new life can be discovered.
> —Joanna Adams

> I am called to bring a word from God to this particular community at this unique moment of history. It has never happened before and it will never happen again.
> Barbara Lundblad

> My old family doctor observed once that health was simply a means to an end. He said, "I have worlds of patients whom I have helped to recover who are still miserable. What people need most is someone to teach them how to live." It seems to me that the ministry offered a direct avenue to this obviously human need.
> —John R. Claypool

• Preach with urgency and conviction.

> I have a deep sense of Isaiah's promise that God's word will not return empty. This sermon is important. It is a matter of life and death for someone today—perhaps for the preacher. Mary Oliver says what I mean in A Poetry Handbook, in which she writes about poems, but I hear sermons: "For poems are not words, after all, but fires for the cold, ropes let down to the lost, something as necessary as bread in the pockets of the hungry. Yes, indeed."
> —Barbara Lundblad

• Speak the truth in love.

> For me preaching is a conversation between God and the
> people as close friends, even more so, lovers. I simply serve
> as the medium of this conversation.
> —Virgilio Elizondo

> Be as pastoral as possible without surrendering ethical
> initiative.
> —William Sloane Coffin

INSTRUCTIONS

A Combination of Gifts and Discipline

Preaching, which requires a great deal of discipline, skill, and commitment on the part of its practitioners, is hard work. The best
preachers not only possess gifts needful for a preaching ministry,
they also work hard at developing those gifts over the course of a
lifetime.

Barbara Brown Taylor, after consulting with a number of lay
people, identifies the following as traits that people in the pew
value in preachers:

> Genuineness in presentation, clarity of thought, appropriate
> humor, faithfulness to the biblical text, attention to the sacred
> dimensions of everyday life and imaginative language.

Taylor encourages anyone who possesses these gifts to consider
whether or not she or he might be recognizing a call to preach.
Joanna Adams reminds us, however, that giftedness takes the
preacher only part of the way home. Hard work and discipline are
its essential partners.

> My advice to people who are considering becoming preach-
> ers is not to do it if you do not intend to work *very hard* at
> it. Preaching requires a great deal of discipline: reading,
> prayer, study, writing, rewriting. I go through each day with
> my eyes and ears open for homiletic possibilities.

In addition to these disciplines, James Henry Harris encourages pastors to remember that the ongoing development of their own spiritual life and moral character is essential for sound preaching.

> The preacher should understand that the call is a call to a
> lifetime of preparation and evaluation of self.

My own experience, while serving as a parish pastor, was that the weekly routine of sermon preparation itself became one of those spiritual disciplines that, over time, encouraged the contin-uing preparation and evaluation of self that Harris advocates. I have only half-joked to my students that there were many weeks in the parish when I felt that the person who was most convicted by my sermon was me.

> Even in my most discouraged moments, I know that the
> privilege of immersing myself in Scripture and applying it to
> the life of a congregation where I am also immersed
> changes me, if no one and nothing else. I take preaching
> seriously because I know it calls me to deeper faithfulness
> and integrity.
> —Arthur P. Boers

The Long View of Preaching

While preaching needs to be taken seriously, one of the mistakes beginning preachers often make is in thinking that everything rides or falls on one sermon—and, consequently, of trying to say everything worth saying in it. I still remember, early in my first parish, one of the dairy farmers in my congregation commenting to me on his way out of church on Sunday morning, "Well, preacher, you sure gave us the whole bale of hay today." It wasn't until I was halfway home that I realized that his comment might not have been meant as a compliment!

Take a long view of the preaching task, and recognize it as a lifetime calling with cumulative effects.

> Trust that one has a lifetime (however long that may be) to say what one is called to say. When I began preaching, I felt compelled to cram all my most important theological ideas into each sermon. Now I am usually content to make one or two points and do that well. Now if a sermon gets too long or promises to be too dense, I divide the sermon into two. While preaching is important, I am not so important that I have to say it all.
>
> —Arthur P. Boers

In a similar vein, Virgilio Elizondo, who celebrates Mass and preaches every day of the week, testifies to the value of brevity in preaching.

> I have learned that sermons do not have to be eternal to be immortal, and some of my best sermons have been my briefest—thirty seconds to one minute. It is much more difficult to prepare a thirty-second sermon than a thirty-minute one.

Preaching Belongs to the Church

The call to proclaim the gospel belongs not to the preacher alone, but to the entire church of Jesus Christ. The preacher stands as one set apart by and for the church to equip and empower its members for their kerygmatic task.

As representatives of the church, faithful preachers do not simply proclaim their own pet theologies or opinions. Rather, they interpret the Scriptures informed by the corporate wisdom of their own denomination and of the church universal.

We are called by the Holy Spirit and the entire Christian church to preach the gospel in that place. We are always representatives of the whole church. I don't become so localized that I forget the pastor is a sign and symbol of the whole church.

—April Larson

Preaching Extends God's Love to the World

Some years ago the World Council of Churches printed a poster that depicted a person with arms wrapped around the world, hugging it fiercely. Like the person in the poster, the faithful pastor is one whose love and compassion extend not only to the church, but also to the entire world.

In telling of his own experience of call, Fred Craddock recounts that there were two complementary parts to it:

> One, a relationship with God sustained by gratitude and prayer, and two, pain over the economic injustices that damaged so many families and lives.

Faithful prophetic preaching is often born when these twin loves—love of God and love of marginalized neighbor—meet.

During his years as pastor of Riverside Church in New York City, William Sloane Coffin earned the reputation as a preacher who was not afraid to tackle the tough political and economic issues of his day with a prophetic voice. His advice to preachers reflects his concern for social justice in proclamation:

> Remember that the neighbor these days needs a helping mind more than a helping hand.
>
> Remember that charity is no substitute for justice, that charity alleviates the effects of poverty while justice seeks to eliminate the causes of it.
>
> Remember that we are called to serve the Lord, not to be servile to our congregations.
>
> Remember to ask always, "What would Jesus have me say?"

THINGS ENCOURAGED AND DISCOURAGED

• Take preaching seriously, but don't take yourself too seriously.

> Recently, I preached a sermon in which I summarized about four years of my thinking on a crucial issue: how we view, understand, perceive, and envision God. It was a good sermon, I thought: compelling scriptures, helpful illustrations and metaphors, and directed to a clear need in the congregation's life. I believed this sermon to be one of my best and most important in years, perhaps ever, and looked forward to delivering it. As circumstances (providence?) would have it, we had one of our lowest attendances ever that Sunday. What I was so eager to deliver was received by only a few.
> —Arthur P. Boers

• Don't tell a congregation what to think.

> Provide a framework for them to think theologically and within the context of the narratives of the Judeo-Christian tradition.
> —Joanna Adams

• Don't mistake the calling to preach with the canonization of personal opinion.

> Our thoughts are not God's thoughts, even on our best days.
> —Robin Meyers

• Don't worry about the results of preaching. Trust those to God.

> While we preachers are called to hone our craft, we do not control the results of proclamation. God works through our best efforts as well as through our poorest offerings. This takes the pressure off of me so I don't presume that everything that happens in the preaching event is dependent on my performance.
>
> —Charles Bugg

> We do not know how sermons bear fruit but trust that they do. Often people get things out of sermons or illustrations that I did not say or intend. Sometimes I smile to myself when this happens and remind myself that God's word shall not return empty, even if I did not put in what it apparently carries!
>
> —Arthur P. Boers

BEST ANSWERS
TO QUESTIONS

• How do I deal with negative criticism in preaching?

> Most of us need affirmative response to our preaching, but I think it is also important for a preacher to be prepared for resistance or criticism. We are not in the pulpit for the sake of the personal response and affirmation we get, but for the glory of God. If one is fundamentally looking for applause, it is best to pursue some other calling.
>
> —J. Philip Wogaman

When I encounter negative criticism, I try to remember that God has called me. I want to be the best me that I can. However, I will always function within the range of certain limits that I have. As much as I want sometimes, I cannot be all things to all people.

—Charles Bugg

There are unhappy moments to be sure. Sometimes I look out at faces that seem at best bored and I wonder, "What's the point?" Sometimes I'm in the middle of a sermon and realize that my sermon is dead. Or once, at the most controversial point of my sermon as a visiting pastor, the whole front row got up and walked out in apparent anger. In such moments, I take comfort in the promise of Isaiah 55:11: "So shall my word be that goes out from my mouth; it shall not return to me empty, but it shall accomplish that which I purpose, and succeed in the thing for which I sent it."

—Arthur P. Boers

• When is preaching more difficult than it should be?

When preaching is an attempt, ever so subtle, to get something for ourselves, it will invariably be a tension-filled enterprise. When preaching is an act of gift-love, then the lilac that willingly shares its fragrance without any thought of who will ever know of the source can be an image of our endeavors. This is what frees preachers to make a present to someone else of what was first of all a gift to them.

—John R. Claypool

• Any wisdom regarding dull and boring preachers?

It is indeed true that, as in the story of Balaam (Numbers 22), the Lord can speak through the mouth of an ass, through the dullest and most plodding of preachers. But this is not an ideal, just a fact.

—Walter Burghardt

CONCLUSION

Recently a seminarian dropped by my office to tell me about his experience of weekly preaching in a small, rural congregation during his summer field education work. His face was aglow as he recounted some of his own "Aha!" discoveries during the sermon preparation process, the blend of discipline and imaginative play that melded to form his own creative writing process, and his awestruck wonder that, through the Spirit's power, his words and insights actually became gospel for his hearers.

"I have to tell you," he said, "that preaching is the hardest work I have ever done in my life. But I also have to tell you that I have never felt more alive than I do in the pulpit on Sunday mornings."

The preachers interviewed for this book readily admit that preaching is hard, tough work, requiring discipline, commitment, and the best resources they can bring to the task. But they also testify to a mystery that resides at the heart of this calling: God uses ordinary human beings to proclaim the riches of an extraordinary gospel and, in the process, brings life-giving joy not only to the hearers, but also to the preacher. It is this reality that causes many preachers, on their better weeks, to want to exult in God's calling as Mary did, and to exclaim with her, "O magnify the Lord with me, and let us exalt God's name together."

BIBLIOGRAPHY

Mulder, John M. "Call" in William H. Willimon and Richard Lischer, *The Concise Encyclopedia of Preaching*. Louisville: Westminster/John Knox Press, 1995, 58–60.

Noren, Carol M. "The Call to Preach" in *The Woman in the Pulpit*. Nashville: Abingdon, 1991, 15–29.

Taylor, Barbara Brown, "Call" and "Vocation" in *The Preaching Life*. Boston: Cowley, 1993, 13–37.

2

GETTING A MESSAGE

Ronald J. Allen

Every semester in my introduction to preaching class some students confess that they are worried about whether they will be able to come up with a fresh focus for the sermon every week. Their hesitation has some justification. Dry spells come in the homiletical life. The preacher sits before a blank computer screen, fidgeting, trying this sentence and that, making one trip after another to the church kitchen to get a fresh cup of coffee.

However, the dry spell is the exception for seasoned pastors who are alive in the gospel, who hold the congregation close to their hearts, who are immersed in the worlds of Scripture and theology, and who are sensitive to the larger culture. Such pastors must frequently choose from among several important sermons that they could develop for a specific Sunday. How does a pastor settle on an energizing focus?

GOALS

• Relate the gospel to life today.

The most important goal is for the preacher to bring a message that relates the gospel of the living God to the community of listeners in the context of the larger culture.

> I see my job as similar to that of a newspaper reporter or columnist. Week by week, I am on the lookout for God's activity in the world. My job is to see it and say it in a way that enables my listeners to see it and say it too.
>
> —Barbara Brown Taylor

The sermon may move from the Bible to life, or from life to the Bible.

> Whichever way it goes, the dialog is the point: God's life and human life, engrossed in deep conversation with one another.
>
> —Barbara Brown Taylor

Monday after Monday, the preacher asks, what does the gospel—the news of God's unconditional love for the world and God's unceasing will for justice in the world as revealed in the stories of Israel and Jesus Christ—offer the church and the wider community? What does the gospel require? The pastor is called to articulate a theological criticism of life and needs to relate the gospel to the life of the community.

> The pastor must take very seriously the needs of a congregation, especially the anxiety, uncertainty, and fears that people have.
>
> —Charles Bugg

Preachers must learn insightful pastoral listening.

James Henry Harris, on behalf of several of our preachers, insists on the priority of Scripture in the process of relating gospel and life.

> The message of the preacher must emanate from the scripture text.

I cannot imagine a Christian sermon that does not engage the Bible. However, a topical or doctrinal sermon need not originate in a text, nor need such sermons be controlled by the exposition of a single biblical passage or theme.

In a side comment, William Sloane Coffin makes a salient point: clergy are called to preach the *gospel*, not the lectionary (or, I might generalize, the Bible). Bishop April Larson observes that the Bible is a collection of primary witnesses to God's actions. The Bible contains paradigms and passages that help us discern the divine presence and leading. Preachers will find themselves relying on their own theological perspective, however, when these witnesses differ with one another or when a biblical passage appears to run against the grain of the gospel.

Several contributors regard the aphorism attributed to Karl Barth as a clear statement of this goal: the preacher enters the pulpit with the Bible in one hand and the newspaper in the other. A preacher's goal is to interpret the full spectrum of life in the light of the gospel.

> There is a temptation in much preaching to focus entirely on personal spiritual life and to ignore the important part of everybody's life that is lived in the wider world.
> —J. Philip Wogaman

• Be clear about how the gospel relates to life.
Clarity is the second goal. The preacher wants the congregation to get the big idea, the proposition.

> Finding a central thrust is one of the marks of a really effective preaching event.
> —John R. Claypool

Further, several of the contributors hint that they hope for the sermon itself to become an *experience* for the community. They want the people both to have a cognitive grasp of the main idea and to feel it in the human gestalt.

> I may have memorized Mark and ransacked Rahner, but if my sermon is simply a masterpiece of Cartesian clarity, I limp along on one leg.
> —Walter Burghardt

A sermon on God's love, for instance, would help listeners understand divine love *and* experience it imaginatively through the medium of the sermon.

INSTRUCTIONS

Theological Reflection

Without doubt, the most important thing a preacher can do toward getting a message across is to recognize the depth of God's love for the preacher and the world and to respond in kind. The preacher needs to interpret this awareness with a lively theology that makes coherent the sense of God, self, human community, and nature. Most preachers today would do well to identify with a theological tradition (for example, fundamental, evangelical, pentecostal, neo-orthodox, post-liberal, liberation, revisionary) and to develop a critical relationship with that tradition, recognizing that preachers never completely accept the standard model but always customize it with their own perspectives.

> A preacher needs a regular discipline of theological reflection. This reflection should include reading, listening to audio tapes, watching video tapes, attending continuing education events, and engaging in theological conversation

with colleagues in the clergy, former teachers, and people in
the congregation.
                              —William Sloane Coffin

No doctor worth his or her salt would close her or his last
medical source upon finishing residency. How dare I cease
seeking understanding of God at ordination?
                              —Walter Burghardt

The preacher also needs a practical theological method to discern the gospel and its implications in biblical texts, in Christian
tradition, in resources outside the Christian house, in relationships and situations from the intimate and personal to the international—even the cosmic. If we don't have such a method, we are
likely to preach our own pet interests with little regard for biblical
or theological content.

Most of us who are preachers have some training in areas
such as psychology and sociology. It's easy to assume that
we have the answers and to twist the biblical text to fit the
contours of our convictions.
                              —Charles Bugg

If I do not listen to God, I will be in great danger of preaching about my own unsuspected and unclaimed idols!
                              —Virgilio Elizondo

My colleague Clark Williamson and I advocate a theological
method centered around three criteria for evaluating every text,
doctrine, practice, and phenomenon.

• Appropriateness to the gospel.
Is a text, doctrine, practice, or phenomenon consistent with the
news of God's unconditional love and God's unremitting call for
justice? If so, what does it offer us? How does it challenge us? If
not, why not? The preacher should describe a more gospel-based
understanding.

• Intelligibility.

Is the text, doctrine, practice, or phenomenon logically consistent with other things that Christians believe and do? Does it make sense in the light of the ways in which the community understands the world today? If not, what are the points of difference? Logical inconsistency or incompatibility with the community's view of the world may cause the preacher to conclude that the text, doctrine, practice, or phenomenon needs to be recast. However, such a discrepancy might also cause us to rethink aspects of what Christians have assumed to be true of our faith and of the world.

• Moral plausibility.

Does the text, doctrine, practice, or phenomenon call for the loving and just treatment of all in its range of concern? If not, what needs to happen for gospel values to be embodied?

As long as we live this side of the eschaton, human finitude will occasionally cause preachers to misname the divine presence and purpose. However, a clear practical theological method can help identify God's activity. Responsible theological criteria can help the preacher discriminate divine truth from scraps of the zeitgeist that blow through the open windows of the study.

Observation of Life

While none of our preachers put it quite this way, they collectively suggest that the preacher could systematically review three arenas for possible suggestions for upcoming messages.

• What is happening in the wider culture that needs to be interpreted by the gospel?

Conditions, dramatic and hardly noticed in the broader setting, may call for homiletical interpretation. For example, William Sloane Coffin suggests that the pastor search for ways to reinterpret religious and secular holidays.

> Give secular holidays religious relevance, and religious holidays secular relevance.

Many clergy, for instance, are deeply offended by the church's past participation in Mother's Day. Yet, if the preacher does not shine some gospel light on Mother's Day (and other days similar to it), the congregation is left to assume that the culture's interpretation of the occasion is the norm for the Christian community. Preachers who are silent about such occasions appear culturally ignorant or irrelevant. A creative preacher can take advantage of the interest stirred by Mother's Day to spark gospel reflection.

David Read remembers a particularly notable occasion when a preacher lost touch with the larger culture.

> The worst sermon I ever heard was delivered in a church in the south of England in September, 1939. The preacher delivered his carefully prepared notes totally unaware of the fact that World War II had just broken out.

- What is happening in the congregation that needs to be interpreted by the gospel?

The preacher conducts an exegesis of the congregation as well as of the biblical text. What is consciously on people's hearts and minds? What are the deeper, perhaps unnamed, issues that need to be addressed from the perspective of the gospel?

> Several years ago, I often found myself involved in pastoral conversations about matters of ethics and personal values. I also sensed similar concerns in the larger culture. I decided to preach a series of sermons entitled "Moral Choices in an Age of Moral Confusion," with the hope that I could address morality without being moralistic. Extra chairs had to be set up in the church parlor because so many people attended worship those weeks. One sermon in the series, "Helping Children Know Right from Wrong" (Psalm 78, Luke 10:21-24), evoked more response than any sermon I have ever preached.
>
> —Joanna Adams

The preacher ought to sometimes speak directly to events that are taking place in the life of the congregation, such as baptism, the breaking of bread, the death of a beloved saint, One Great Hour of Sharing.

- What is happening in the life of the preacher that needs to be interpreted by the gospel?

> Bring the text to the context of your life, and your life to the text.
> —April Larson

> Take seriously listening to the Holy Spirit by prayerfully paying attention to Scriptures, *one's own life*, the needs of one's parishioners, and the life of one's congregation.
> —Arthur P. Boers

> The best source for a sermon may be a conversation in the waiting room at the doctor's office, or a scene glimpsed from the windows of a city bus. It is not these encounters alone that make them worth preaching but what they and the word of God have to say to one another.
> —Barbara Brown Taylor

> Pay attention to what *inspires* you, rather than just what appears to be a conventional sermon source.
> —Robin Meyers

Planning in Advance

Thomas Long will say more about the details of sermon planning as it applies to sermon preparation in the next chapter. Our preachers, however, are convinced that careful planning is extremely helpful to the process of getting a message. A long range plan frees the preacher from the desperation of scratching for a sermon from one week to the next. Long range planning also allows future sermons to compost in the preacher's mind and heart.

When the pastor starts to prepare the sermon, the compost pile is full of insight that has been long and quietly fermenting but is only now coming to consciousness.

THINGS ENCOURAGED AND DISCOURAGED

Things Encouraged

• Make preaching a way of life.

Think of the ministerial vocation not as a job but, with Barbara Brown Taylor, as the preaching life. Some of the best preparation for the sermon takes place as preachers immerse themselves fully in day-to-day living.

> My sermon is all around me, from rising to retiring: the people I meet, the stories I hear, the incidents I observe, the hospitals and jails I visit, books, articles, TV—the hurts and fears, the joys and hopes of my people.
> —Walter Burghardt

> Keep a journal. Write in forms other than the sermonic. Try your hand at poetry. Don't forget that nothing matches live music and live theater for moving the soul. Pay attention to *little* things, and get yourself out of the way (self-consciousness thwarts revelation). Take walks and notice the sky.
> —Robin Meyers

• Develop a life of prayer and Bible reading outside the immediate anxiety of preparing a sermon.

> Giving myself to disciplined and prayerful reading of Scripture gives me the eye I bring to all else I read and see. This is far more than finding a text for Sunday and doing an

exegesis of that text. I am talking about a way of being formed as a Christian and as a preacher. Out of this reservoir one preaches particular texts but is never guilty of proof-texting, which comes from "using" the Bible for sermons.
—Fred Craddock

Praying, especially for others, sensitizes the preacher.

Being people of prayer affects all our lives in that we learn to *pay attention* to others, ourselves, stories we hear, the life of our congregation.
—Arthur P. Boers

• Be aware of theological and cultural presuppositions.
Become critical of the theological lenses through which we interpret the Bible, Christian theology, and the Christian life.

In our ordination, we commit ourselves to preach the biblical witness to God in Christ *as interpreted* by the ecumenical creeds and the confessions of our particular traditions.
—John Vannorsdall

In addition to formal theological traditions, preachers interpret Christian witness through the lenses of race, gender, class, education, philosophy, political orientation, local custom, and a host of other factors. The preacher needs to become aware, and critical, of these qualities both to guard against their inappropriate intrusion into the gospel message and as live points of contact with the gospel.

• Keep secondary sources secondary.
At the beginning of sermon preparation, respond to the biblical text, (or a doctrine, an issue, or a situation) before turning to secondary sources.

Each time I am to preach, I engage the four scriptures that are proposed in the lectionary and ask first, "What do these

words say to me?" I read them slowly and meditatively and keep careful note of the impressions that they evoke, the questions that are raised, and the affirmations that I find myself receiving. Having allowed the scriptures to resonate with me, I then consult second and third opinions in terms of the commentaries and theological works that abound.
                                            —John R. Claypool

Commentaries should be your last step instead of your first because most commentaries soften the ambiguities and challenges present in the text. One commentary that cuts through our cultural presuppositions is *The Women's Bible Commentary.*
                                            —April Larson

Even the best commentators are often unaware of their own biases. Preachers need to be aware of such prejudices. Furthermore, scholars in Cambridge, New York City, Durham, and Claremont do not always have the last interpretive word on a passage. If a preacher generates an exegetical possibility that is not immediately confirmed in a commentary, I urge the preacher to stay with that possibility long enough to check out its plausibility through independent investigation.

• Work toward a pulpit that is both pastoral and prophetic.

I believe that effective preaching balances the pastoral and the prophetic.
                                            —Charles Bugg

Our preachers agree with Charles Bugg. However, the pastoral and the prophetic are not diametric opposites. All preaching is ultimately pastoral in that all preaching aims to build up the community. The goal of prophetic preaching is precisely this: to build up the community by calling it to account for injustice, prejudice, and oppression.

Things Discouraged

• Don't offer simplistic solutions to complex situations.

> We must get behind what is happening to the very roots of why things are happening—violence, child abuse, crime, increasing poverty, broken homes, hate-filled society, spirit of vengeance masked by demands for legal justice, treating immigrants like criminals for the crime of being poor. Why are we losing concern for the common good? We must address the roots of evil and sin if we are to offer true salvation.
>
> —Virgilio Elizondo

Today's preacher must be able to analyze the various social, political, economic, and philosophical systems that organize our worlds.

• Do not approach every event in life as a source of potential sermons.

> I would urge upon any preacher the widest possible reading and a wide-eyed energy for life. But not just to get sermon material, being constantly on the prowl. There are sermons in the stones, but not if you approach the quarry in your robe!
>
> —Robin Meyers

The preacher who searches every experience for the thing that will preach soon loses sight of the experience itself.

• Do not passively accept the beginning and ending points of biblical passages as they are designated by the lectionary.

> Be attentive to the commas! What's been left out, and why?
>
> —Barbara Lundblad

The lectionary sometimes edits out material that is troubling (and, therefore, often the best place to begin a homily) or important to understanding the pericope. When getting a message from the lectionary, the preacher's first task is to confirm the proper beginning and ending points of the passage.

- Do not think that there is one perfect way to get a sermon message.

> There can be no one rule that fits all in how to best select the sources of a message.
> —Arthur P. Boers

Every preacher, every congregation, and every situation is different.

BEST ANSWERS
TO QUESTIONS

- Should I preach directly on controversial issues? Or should I pussyfoot around them?

J. Philip Wogaman does not mince words.

> I can understand why some preachers and professors of homiletics counsel us to avoid dealing directly with the social issues in sermons—allowing people to arrive at their own conclusions. But I am afraid the conclusion people most readily arrive at when we avoid issues is that Christian faith really is irrelevant to the particulars.

• Is it permissible for preachers to use their own life experience as a source for sermon messages?
Robin Meyers finds it not only permissible, but desirable.

> People have a right to know that you study the Scriptures. But they also want to know that you wash dishes, make love, and sometimes have trouble sleeping.

Indeed, the preacher's own life can be the occasion of revelation. However, another of our preachers states a wise caution regarding the use of personal experience in preaching.

> I do not preach Virgilio Elizondo but pray that, through me, Jesus of Nazareth might be able to speak today.
> —Virgilio Elizondo

While the experience of the minister can serve as a resource for the sermon, the preacher needs to respect the confidence of family, friends, and parishioners. Some things are sufficiently private and personal that they ought not be aired in public.

• How can I remember all the good ideas that I have for sermons?
A preacher needs a system to keep track of the insights and experiences that might one day inspire a sermon. A preacher might keep a notebook, a supply of 3 x 5 cards in a pocket or purse, a drawer to stuff pages from *The Christian Century* into, a pad and paper on the nightstand and in the car, a file on a computer disk, or a bookmark to locate important passages. Periodically, the preacher can review the growing collection and sort the items that seem promising after sitting awhile from the ideas that have lost their magnetism.

• Must a preacher follow the lectionary texts every Sunday?
Certainly not. The lectionary and other forms of long-range planning are the servants, not the tyrants, of the pulpit.

There are weeks when something so extraordinary, perhaps catastrophic, has occurred that the preacher who doesn't respond to that event in his or her sermon allows that day's preaching to become irrelevant for most people who come. Heads shake wonderingly as people head for their cars. Words such as *coward* and *idiot* come to mind, though they are seldom spoken.

—John Vannorsdall

After the tragic bombing in Oklahoma City, there was a deep need in our congregation to directly address that event, so I tailored my sermon accordingly. On another occasion, a serious problem had developed in the life of our church that required homiletical attention.

—J. Philip Wogaman

• Is it permissible to preach another person's sermon?
Only under exceptional circumstances. For example, a church anniversary may be well-served by a sermon that was delivered in the formative years of the denomination or congregation. However, if so, the preacher should clearly acknowledge the source of the sermon and should explain why he or she selected this task.

• Must every sermon have a biblical text?
Expository preaching should be the typical pattern. However, Lowell Erdahl finds that revelation is not confined to the Bible.

Although the Scriptures are the primary source of our message, it is also true that all truth is God's truth, and our sermons are rightly enriched by wisdom from wherever we find it.

From time to time, a preacher might take a play or a movie or a song or an event as a text.

CONCLUSION

Experienced pastors often generate more material than can be used in a single sermon. Leaving particular insights on the desk in the study feels like leaving a child alongside the road. At such times, a pastor can remember that preaching is part of an ongoing, multi-faceted ministry.

> The glory of parish ministry is that all of the work does not have to be done in a single day. You will have other opportunities to share with these people. Therefore, deciding—in light of what you know about them and about the moment in history in which you find yourself—the main gifts that you would like to give is at the foundation of the kind of ministry that really does enrich and bless.
>
> —John R. Claypool

BIBLIOGRAPHY

Allen, Ronald J. *Preaching the Topical Sermon.* Louisville: Westminster/John Knox Press, 1992.

Allen, Ronald J. *The Teaching Sermon.* Nashville: Abingdon Press, 1995, "Plans for Systematic Teaching from the Pulpit," pp. 126–40.

Allen, Ronald J. "Why Preach from Passages in the Bible?" in *Preaching as a Theological Task: World, Gospel, Scripture,* edited by Thomas G. Long and Edward Farley. Louisville: Westminster/John Knox Press, 1996. Reviews emerging debate on whether preaching from a singular biblical pericope is an optimum paradigm.

Carl, William J. *Preaching Christian Doctrine*. Philadelphia: Fortress Press, 1984.

Craddock, Fred B. *Preaching*. Nashville: Abingdon Press, 1985, pp. 69–169, "The Life of Study," "Interpretation: The Listeners," "Interpretation: The Text," "Interpretation: Between Text and Listener," "Qualities to be Sought in a Sermon."

Taylor, Barbara Brown *The Preaching Life*. Boston: Cowley Publications, 1993.

3

PATTERNS IN SERMONS

Thomas G. Long

When most people are asked to do advance planning about some matter they will usually say, "Let me check my calendar." For preachers, however, life is not so simple; they are obliged to reply, "Let me check my calendars," since as many as four different calendars lie open on the preacher's desk.

First, there is the *liturgical* calendar. Virtually every congregation—whether high church or low, city or rural, large or small, Protestant or Catholic—follows at least some of the contours of the Christian liturgical year. Christmas and Easter, Advent and Lent, Pentecost and Epiphany—each season and festival brings its own themes and demands to the preaching task. Moreover, many preachers follow one of the denominational or ecumenical lectionaries, which are calibrated to the liturgical calendar.

Second, the *ecclesiastical* calendar brings an array of denominational and churchly events, such as stewardship season, theological education Sunday, race relations Sunday, World Communion Sunday, mission emphasis season, peacemaking Sunday, and the like.

Third, the *civic* calendar includes not only the slate of *public holidays* (like Thanksgiving, Independence Day, and Martin Luther King Jr.'s Birthday), but also the holy days of other faiths (such as Yom Kippur) and the days and seasons, some seemingly playful and frivolous, that nonetheless mark the rhythms and rests of the larger secular culture (like Mother's Day, back-to-school season, Halloween, and Super Bowl Sunday).

Finally, there is the *local church* calendar. Every congregation has its own unique docket of anniversaries, homecomings, festivals, and program emphases that deserve attention in worship, sometimes in the sermon. For example, the children's choir in your church may be scheduled to sing a brief cantata in worship next March. For the church across the street, this March Sunday will simply be the fourth Sunday in Lent, but for your congregation, it will be the day when the pews are filled with parents and grandparents (some of whom are in worship only on this occasion) and when children will be in leadership roles in worship. The sermon that day should not ignore this special and particular context.

Given these many calendars and their compelling—sometimes competing—pulls on the pulpit, how should the schedule of preaching be set? What forces should influence the preacher's planning? What themes should emerge? What patterns should become visible in our week-in-week-out program of preaching? To establish a responsible program of congregational preaching, we must first identify the goals we are trying to achieve.

GOALS

• Have a systematic but flexible plan for your preaching.

Good preaching requires good planning. The slapdash method of opening the Bible and the newspaper on Monday morning and musing, "What shall I preach about next Sunday?" is inefficient and exhausting to the preacher. Slapdash preparation also communicates, by its very aimlessness, randomness, and susceptibility to being blown by every wind that whistles through the culture, an unsteady grasp of the gospel. Moreover, homiletical short order cooks who rifle through the pantry trying to scare something up for next Sunday's sermon inevitably undernourish the congregations who depend on them for a balanced diet of teaching and preaching.

On the other hand, it is possible to be too exacting and rigid in sermon planning. Good planning requires not only a sense of direction but also freedom and flexibility. Sometimes unexpected events of such size and moment occur that they demand response from the pulpit. When word arrived on a Friday afternoon in 1963 that President John Kennedy had been assassinated, many preachers had already finished preparing their sermons for the coming Sunday. The good preachers, though, did not preach those sermons unchanged, but went back to the study to refashion and revise, or perhaps even to start afresh, so that they could respond with a timely gospel word addressed to the national crisis.

David Read advances yet another reason for flexibility in sermon planning: the congregation's questions about and responses to one sermon may suggest the direction for a following sermon.

> I have found that it is better not to plan too completely, since often one sermon will suggest follow-up treatments of related topics.

A comprehensive plan will be thoughtfully attentive to all four calendars, carefully plotting the cadences of the congregation's life, but allowing room for the unexpected event and the refreshing intrusion of the Spirit.

• Strive for variety.
Left to our own devices, most of us who preach would fall into a numbing monotony, employing pet themes, worn transitions, and predictable sermon structures, too easily slipping into the habit of pouring this week's gelatin into last week's mold. The gospel is not monochromatic but a rich palette of colors, and faithful preaching must display the full rainbow. Our sermon planning, then, must provide not only for a variety of themes and issues but also for variation in sermon styles and forms.

• Ensure breadth.

If good preaching is varied in theme and style, it is also comprehensive and broad. The Christian faith is not a single point on the
compass, but a panoramic embrace of human life and meaning.
Think for a moment of a basic Christian creed, the Apostles' Creed
for example, and visualize this creed as a set of theological boxes,
a grid of possible preaching categories. Now, what if you were to
file each week's sermon into its proper box in the creed? One
week, say, the sermon is on the creation and ecology, and it would
go into the box labeled "I believe in God . . . maker of heaven and
earth." The next week, the sermon is on the difficulty of forgiveness in human relationships, and it gets placed in the "I believe in
. . . the forgiveness of sins" box. At the end of a year, which boxes
would be filled to overflowing and which would be scarce, or even
empty? Bare spaces in the grid are signs of a preaching range that is
too narrow. Good preaching, like painting a canvas, not only aims
at variety and color but also coverage.

• Seek depth.

A preacher can dazzle a congregation with variety and cover a
great deal of territory with multiple themes but never go to the
heart of any concern, theological or pastoral. In a world of instant
analysis, a culture where television pundits attempt to sum up
intricacies in sound bites, the preacher conveys an important witness by confessing mystery and refusing to sum up every issue in
a single, brief sermon. Some topics require that the preacher
return again and again to the theme, exposing greater and greater
complexity. Careful planning allows the river of one's preaching to
move here swift and full of white-water excitement and there slow
and still, with power and great depth.

• Respond to the living needs of the congregation.

Every preacher stands in a unique spot. No other preacher looks
out at the same improbable mix of human personalities, eccen-
tricities, gifts, and longings that you do. Therefore, no one-size-
fits-all plan for preaching will be suited to your congregation, and
every preaching pattern must be cut to fit the specific needs of

these people. This does not mean, though, that a preacher should simply preach what people want to hear or take a vote on sermon topics. We are called to preach what people *need*, which is not to be equated with what people *desire*. But sermons are not treatises carved in oak; they are gospel words addressed to *these* people in *this* place trying on *this* day to be faithful to *this* aspect of God's call. All sound sermon planning recognizes that good preaching is inevitably very local and, therefore, must be responsive to the needs of a particular people.

INSTRUCTIONS

Where to Begin

Good sermon planning takes time, thought, and prayer. Indeed, preachers could well think of sermon planning in long-range, middle-range, and short-range terms.

As for long-range planning, Fred Craddock advises an annual homiletical retreat of several days to plan one's preaching, a practice that J. Philip Wogaman follows:

> I am given two or three weeks, usually at the beginning of the summer, to hole up somewhere with abundant reference materials and other reading, and at the end of that time I hope to have a basic outline of the year in hand. That will include a specific title and a brief synopsis of what I hope to do with the sermon, along with the Old and New Testament scripture readings and suggested hymns.

The best starting point in long-range planning for a program of preaching is with the liturgical calendar, the Christian year. As we have noted, this is not the preacher's only calendar, but it is the *basic* one, the essential framework into which all other themes and emphases will be fit. Then the other calendars—ecclesiastical, civic, and local church—can be overlaid onto the governing pattern of the Christian year. Of course, the use of multiple calendars inevitably creates tensions and conflicts, and judgment calls must be made, but setting the Christian year as the main framework allows the gospel to be the primary shaping force.

> I am not big on relating to the secular calendar, but when Sunday falls on the Fourth of July, I think it would be foolish to ignore it. At the same time, I don't think it necessary to preach about motherhood on every Mother's Day.
> —Lowell Erdahl

If long-range planning thinks in terms of months, seasons, and perhaps a whole year of sermons, middle-range planning looks ahead four to six weeks. Most of us find it impossible to do creative brooding and thinking about a whole year's worth of sermons at once, but we can work actively on five or six sermons at a time. The best strategy is to plant what the old-timers in homiletics used to call a homiletical garden, a patch where a few sermons are cultivated to maturity. One good way to do this is to do some preliminary exegetical work on the biblical texts for the next few weeks' sermons and place notes for each in a separate file folder. Then, make use of the spare moments in the day (while on hold on the phone or waiting for the next appointment to arrive) to browse through these folders, thus keeping fresh in mind the basic themes of the upcoming five or six sermons. As you go about your work and leisure, ideas, images, illustrations, and quotations that relate to these sermons will occur in your reading, experience, and thinking. When this happens, scribble a reminder on a piece of paper and drop it in the appropriate file. When the time comes to work on that sermon, the chances are good that the folder will be stuffed with a confetti of resources, reflections, and approaches.

In terms of short-range planning, the preacher should develop a weekly routine for sermon preparation and stick to it—in short, develop a good homiletical habit. One effective pattern is to work hard on the sermon for a few hours early in the week—Monday or, at the latest, Tuesday—and then put the sermon aside for a day or two. This allows time for the basic ideas to ferment in the imagination. Then later in the week, the preacher can return to the sermon to develop the initial ideas and move toward the final crafting process.

Using the Lectionary

For many preachers, beginning the sermon planning process with the Christian year also entails starting with the lectionary, a schedule of assigned scriptural lessons matched to the liturgical calendar. As Walter Burghardt put it:

> I advise preachers, whenever possible, to base their sermons on the lectionary. Why? Because such preaching is more likely to stay close to God's revealed Word, follow the gospel story through a whole liturgical year, and compel the preacher to link today's human problems to Scripture.

Barbara Brown Taylor adds:

> I have been a lectionary preacher for so long that I fumble when I have to pick a text out of thin air for a special occasion. When I pick the text, it seems that I am shopping for a piece of scripture that will back up what I already know I want to say. When the text picks me, I know I am in for a discovery. The lectionary provides me with breadth and discipline I lack on my own, and my sermons are fresher with it than without it. The liturgical year provides a natural pattern for preaching.

Not every church tradition is at home with the lectionary, however. Indeed, the use of a lectionary would seem at first to be a dividing point between preachers who are part of the more structured liturgical traditions, where the lectionary is firmly in place, and those from the free church traditions, where lectionary use has not been an established practice. The differences, however, are not as dramatic as one might expect. A free-church preacher who does careful planning ends up constructing a kind of local lectionary, selecting appropriate scriptures for Christmas, Easter, and so on, and ensuring that a range of passages from the Gospels, epistles, Old Testament, and other books of the Bible is included. Charles Bugg, a preacher in a free-church tradition (Baptist), states that:

> While I do not use the lectionary, I do try to take seriously preaching that prepares the congregation for pivotal times such as Christmas, Easter, and Pentecost.

For their part, almost all of the more liturgically oriented preachers report that they must also localize the lectionary, modifying the readings in various ways and departing from them altogether from time to time.

> My own tradition (Lutheran) is guided by the rhythm of the church year and the readings of the Revised Common Lectionary. The lectionary readings provide the basic outlines for my preaching from Sunday to Sunday. But, the lectionary has limitations. Especially during the long after-Pentecost season, preachers should consider alternate lectionaries and should also be attentive to non-liturgical days, such as Martin Luther King Jr.'s Birthday.
> —Barbara Lundblad

> The lectionary is not favorable to marginalized groups in society. So, although I use the lectionary, I find times to include important texts that speak to those people who have been left out of the lectionary. Also, some of the most important texts that demonstrate how "unsafe" our God is are not in the lectionary. The preacher must find ways to address these texts and preach them, too.
> —April Larson

Another common dilemma among lectionary preachers involves the question of which of the biblical texts assigned for each Sunday should be preached. The lectionary itself has a slight tilt toward the Gospel text, but, as John Claypool maintains, "To always preach from the Gospel (or from the Old Testament or the epistle) would be a mistake. We are commissioned 'to share the whole counsel of God' with our people. . . ." If it is a mistake to gravitate always to the Gospel text, it is also a blunder to try to preach on all four of the readings for a week. While cross-referencing among the readings is sometimes desirable, most of the time it is better to pick only one of the texts as the basis for the sermon. Trying to blend all of the weekly lessons into a homiletic milkshake eliminates the rich and distinctive flavoring each text alone has to offer.

Achieving Variety and Breadth

Variety and breadth are, first of all, products of diverse biblical texts. If a preacher has the courage to delve seriously into the multi-faceted wealth of the Bible, the resulting sermons will display a fascinating diversity and scope. Using the lectionary or some other method that ensures a wide range of biblical texts for preaching is a good start toward bringing about variety and breadth in preaching, but it is only a beginning. The preacher must also remember that a biblical text is not a jar with an idea inside, waiting to be plucked out and preached. A text, rather, is like a large and lavishly furnished room. It can be entered through several doorways and, once inside, the preacher can experience this environment in many ways. A single text, then, affords multiple preaching possibilities. I know of one preacher who preached at a conference four evenings in a row on the same biblical passage, and each of the sermons, though faithful to the text, was dramatically different in content, structure, and style. John R. Claypool describes several of the possible approaches he might take with a text:

> There are many occasions when a straight exegetical unpacking of a particular text is appropriate. Here the sermon is structured according to the flow of the text. On other occasions, I simply tell the story that is described in the biblical material and allow the inherent truth that is already there to come to life without a great deal of elaboration. On

> other occasions, I am unashamedly confessional in the way
> I do the gift-giving task. I personally believe that what has
> happened to us can also happen *through* us.

Virgilio Elizondo achieves variety in his preaching by paying special attention to what he calls "core images" in the biblical text "around which I can tie the message that seems to be appropriate for this congregation in this particular time and place." Barbara Lundblad agrees, noting that the Isaiah texts for Advent give a medley of "strong images (spears to plowshares, a shoot growing from a stump, flowers blooming in the desert)," which suggests the possibility that "the preacher may choose to do a series of image sermons." She goes on to say, "Hymns, artwork, the eucharistic prayer, and the bulletin cover can enhance the image developed in the sermon."

Variety and breadth come not only from diverse biblical texts but also from the congregation's changing context. For example, suppose that a preacher is developing a sermon on the famous passage in 1 Corinthians 12 about "varieties of gifts but the same Spirit." If the congregation is going through a season of discouragement, convinced they have no mission and no future, then the emphasis of the sermon will fall on the text's promise that God surely gives to the church "varieties of gifts." But if the congregation is currently engaged in a divisive, knock-down church fight, with one group bickering with another, then the sermon will move in the direction of affirming that it is "the same Spirit" who moves us all toward the common good. The sermon is a product of the interaction between a rich, multi-faceted text and an ever-changing cultural and congregational context.

Seeking Depth

The gospel addresses the profundities of human life, not merely the surfaces. Preachers, then, should ensure that their sermons do not fasten on gimmicks, novelties, or breezy themes at the expense of hard topics, difficult questions, and anguished struggles. A great teacher of preaching, Edmund Steimle, used to warn his students that a sermon is not "a neat package tied up with a bow, but more like the rings on the surface of a lake when a swimmer has dived into deep water."

Steering away from difficult biblical texts can be a missed opportunity to move to a deeper level.

> There are times when the lectionary texts are so obscure, contrary to my personal understanding, or seemingly irrelevant that I become angry with frustration. Then I become stubborn, determined not to be beaten by a biblical text. This stubbornness often results in a sermon that engages the hearers and evokes for me, and perhaps for some members of the congregation, a larger understanding of the biblical witness.
>
> —John Vannorsdall

William Sloane Coffin challenges preachers to achieve depth by embracing the political dimensions of life.

> Before elections, it is important to show the relationship between politics and morality, to show that an issue is not less spiritual for being political and that personal morality doesn't challenge the status quo while social morality does.

John Vannorsdall shares Coffin's view of the relationship between the gospel and social and political issues, but he issues an important warning:

> There is a difference between preaching on social issues and preaching the gospel in ways that illumine social issues and our complicities and responsibilities. I am offended by the first, because it is a misuse of the pulpit. I affirm the second in spite of the difficulties and my limitations.

A single sermon lasts but a few minutes, hardly enough time to treat any topic in depth. Several of our preachers overcome this problem by occasionally developing a connected series of sermons. Lowell Erdahl, for example, has preached an Advent series called "Christ Was Born for This," which explored, at a depth not possible in a single sermon, the purposes of the incarnation. He also preached a Lenten series "on comments by critics of Christ that unwittingly witnessed to the gospel," such as "this man receives sinners" and "he saved others, he cannot save himself."

Robin Meyers also develops sermon series, sometimes around a biblical form, like parable or beatitude, sometimes on a theological theme, and sometimes developed by preaching through a book of the Bible.

> What they accomplish is a sense of continuity and connection. In a media-dominated era, they are like a miniseries, communicating a sense of "to be continued." If the sermons are truly hooked together and built upon one another, the listeners seem to feel both complimented and motivated. I have seen parishioners go to great lengths to catch up and stay current with a sermon series.

Charles Bugg also favors the occasional sermon series, but he advises that a series should not be too extended, perhaps eight sermons as a maximum, and that each sermon should be able to stand on its own apart from the others. "This is important," he maintains, "in a time when we cannot assume the presence of everybody on every Sunday."

THINGS ENCOURAGED AND DISCOURAGED

Things Encouraged

- Take a homiletical retreat each year to plan your preaching.
- In planning a year's preaching, begin with the liturgical calendar, but also pay attention to the ecclesiastical, civic, and local church calendars.
- Approach biblical texts with an open mind and an inquisitive spirit, seeking the many possibilities for preaching that each text supplies.

- Develop an occasional sermon series that explores a book of the Bible, a theological concept, a significant pastoral question, or a biblical theme.

Things Discouraged

- Don't employ a haphazard, "What shall I preach next Sunday?" approach to sermon planning.
- Don't fall into the habit of building every sermon the same way.
- Don't try to blend the lectionary texts for a given Sunday into one giant preaching passage.
- Don't avoid hard texts, difficult questions, or demanding political and social issues in preaching.

BEST ANSWERS TO QUESTIONS

- I think that secular festivals like Independence Day, Father's Day, and Memorial Day are disruptive intrusions into the church's witness. Shouldn't we simply ignore them from the pulpit?

You are probably right that, most of the time, these occasions are disruptions, but for that very reason they should not be ignored. If such times and seasons have disruptive power, then this points to something important at work in the larger culture. If we object to a Hallmark greeting card view of Father's Day, then we should engage that view from the pulpit. We should challenge it, acknowledge what value it may have, and provide an alternative view of fathering and parenting from the point of view of the gospel.

- What about topical sermons? I was taught that a sermon should always be biblical. Aren't topical sermons non-biblical by definition?

It depends. Some topical sermons do not come anywhere near a biblical text, but others spring solidly from biblical material. Walter Burghardt suggests that a preacher could stick to the lectionary and still preach a good topical sermon series. If the series were on the theme of justice, for example, the preacher would go to each week's lessons, Burghardt suggests, asking what this passage teaches us about biblical justice. Put that way, the preacher would find that just about every biblical passage is about some aspect of justice.

- Most of the time I am a lectionary preacher, but sometimes I feel hemmed in by the lectionary. Are there times and ways that are better than others to take an occasional vacation from the lectionary?

> Given the general lack of biblical knowledge in our congregations, that portion of ordinary time between Pentecost and Advent could well be spent leading one's listeners through large, continuous narratives of the Bible.
> —Fred Craddock

> I may go after some of the texts that the lectionary ignores. I can imagine a series on the minor prophets, on New Testament evangelists, on dreamers in the Bible, on Proverbs, or on the Song of Solomon. It would also be interesting to spend a year on the four great themes of creation, fall, judgment, and redemption.
> —Barbara Brown Taylor

- Can you suggest any ways for a preacher to expand the repertoire of sermon patterns and styles?

> Reading a short story each week would be an excellent discipline for every preacher, for the short story is the artform closest to that of the sermon.
> —John R. Claypool

- For the sake of being creative and gaining interest, should we always seek to preach on surprising and unfamiliar texts and topics?

> It is a good idea to keep making fresh what is familiar. For example, preach a series on the Lord's Prayer, the Sunday liturgy, or the Twenty-third Psalm.
>   —William Sloane Coffin

• What about the use of drama and first-person sermons?

> Sermons in which I speak as though I am the biblical character are refreshing for the congregation, especially when they occur about once every five years.
>   —John Vannorsdall

> I am halfway through a sermon series on Søren Kierkegaard's criticisms of official Christianity. Each Sunday I bring a straight-back Danish chair draped with a scarf and cap and set it next to the pulpit. It's S.K.'s chair, a reminder of our imaginary guest.
>   —Robin Meyers

BIBLIOGRAPHY

Eslinger, Richard L., "Church Year and Preaching," in William H. Willimon and Richard Lischer, editors, *Concise Encyclopedia of Preaching*. Louisville: Westminster/John Knox Press, 1995.

Long, Thomas G. and Neely McCarter, editors, *Preaching in and Out of Season*. Louisville: Westminster/John Knox Press, 1990.

McClure, John S., *The Roundtable Pulpit: Where Leadership and Preaching Meet*. Nashville: Abingdon Press, 1995.

4

COLLECTING SUPPORTIVE MATERIAL

William H. Willimon

In the inaugural Beecher Lectures (1872), Henry Ward Beecher extolled the need for good illustration in sermons and confessed to his own growth in this facility.

> Illustrations are as natural to me as breathing, I use fifty now to one in the early years of my ministry. For the first six or eight years, perhaps, they were comparatively few and far apart. But I developed a tendency that was latent in me, and educated myself in that respect; and that, too, by study and practice, by hard thought, and by a great many trials, both with the pen, and extemporaneously by myself, when I was walking here and there. Whatever I have gained in that direction is largely the result of education. You need not, therefore, be discouraged if it does not come to you immediately.

Illustrations are the lifeblood of our sermons. They make the truth vivid, concrete, engaging. The move from biblical text to contemporary congregational context occurs along the path provided by stories, illustrations, analogies, examples, and images.

This we know. Yet how does a preacher find, preserve, and relocate illustrative material? The apt illustration—found while wandering leisurely through some book, jotted on a scrap of paper, stuffed in a desk drawer—where is it when we need it?

Moreover, the skillful illustration of sermons is more than a technical matter of finding, keeping, and finding again. It is also a gift for seeing the connections between the gospel and life.

GOALS

• Use appropriate illustrations.

A good illustration fits. When utilized it evokes recognition, assent, and engagement in the hearer. Our preachers agreed that illustrations from everyday life, including the experiences of the preacher, are preferable to those from literature, history, or biography. Generally speaking, the well-read preacher is probably a well-spoken preacher. Reading puts us in conversation with other communicators, others who struggle to make contact with the lives of people through words.

Yet there was a strong feeling among our preachers that good illustration begins in the cultivation of one's own experiences as a source for sermon illustration.

> I would advise preachers to depend less on clippings and quotations and more on careful, keen observation of their own lives and the lives of those around them. The sheer volume of material for preaching can now be almost overwhelming, especially with the advent of more pulpit publications and the mountain of books that the average seminary student will unpack in her or his first office. But I continue to believe that people want to hear from a person, not just from a personality, however well informed. People are looking for more than cleverness. They are looking for authenticity—someone who is transparent to the gospel.
>
> —Robin Meyers

Observation leading to good illustration probably begins in the preacher's conviction that his or her life is eventful, typical, and a place where God meets the world.

Some time ago, Martin Copenhaver contrasted my way of illustrating sermons with that of Harry Emerson Fosdick. He noted that Fosdick used as many as twenty illustrative quotes per sermon. On the other hand, I rarely quoted anyone or cited any experience other than my own. Copenhaver concluded that Fosdick bolstered his sermons with quotes from secular authorities, thus demonstrating that his sermons were relevant, well informed, and in dialogue with culture. My sermons appeared to be more concerned with the internal edification of the church and the confrontation with Scripture rather than culture. This suggests that the source, type, and number of our illustrations is a function of the goals of our preaching and the source of our homiletical authority.

• Develop an eye for illustrative material.
There is never any moment in life when a preacher is not, in a broad sense, engaged in sermon preparation and, therefore, illustration collection. I once heard an author say, "Nothing bad ever happens to a writer." By this statement she meant that even life's worst experiences provide material. Our goal ought to be to cultivate that consciousness whereby we are open to illustrations.

> By all means, develop the ability to reflect on life at times when you are not conscious of sermon development at all. Go to movies and enjoy them as art, not as potential sermon material. Observe children, read for pleasure, and take the road less traveled from time to time.
> —Robin Meyers

• Develop a storage and retrieval system.
The development of some systematic means of collecting, preserving, and retrieving illustrative material is one of our main goals. Barbara Brown Taylor confesses her own frustration in filing and finding:

> I have never found a filing system that works, which is probably fine since articles and ideas get stale faster than bread. In general, I reach for supportive material from current events in my life, the congregation's life, and the life of the world.

I like her point about illustrations going stale. A major problem encountered with old illustrations is that a really good illustration gleaned from the media or other preachers, if it is really good, is quickly overused. In our chapel, over a two-month period, we heard the same story in three guest preachers' sermons. If an illustration or metaphor arises from your own experience, you need not worry about this problem.

In spite of Taylor's cautions, however, there are many times when an older illustration can be used. Robin Meyers expresses the frustration many of us preachers feel when, on the eve of a sermon we ask ourselves, "Where is that story I read somewhere on this scripture?"

> Whatever method you choose to organize your stories, illustrations, and other sermon material, be sure that you can retrieve it. There is nothing more frustrating than not being able to find something.

Any system for filing and retrieving sermon illustrations is better than none.

INSTRUCTIONS

Connecting the Biblical Text with Life

The beginning of effective, faithful illustration is engagement with the biblical text. We do not search for cute, interesting, or vivid illustration. We search for a way to connect the biblical text with our congregations. The very word *illustration* means literally to throw light on something. A good illustration helps to enlighten the biblical text. Warning: if a story or image is strong and memorable, it is able to take over a sermon, to stick in the minds of listeners. A primary question to ask is, does this illustration illuminate *this* text?

Therefore, we need a multifaceted engagement with the text as the first phase of sermon preparation.

> I believe the best way to begin collecting supportive material is by reading the text out loud and paying attention to the associations it evokes. How do I feel when I hear it? When was the last time I felt that way? What is the connection? What book, movie, event, or conversation does the text bring to mind?
>
> Once I have established my own kinship with the text, I spend hours with commentaries—not help sheets for preachers but scholarly texts on the passages at hand, with Kittel's *Theological Dictionary of the New Testament* on hand for word work. For Old Testament texts, I use a modern commentary on the Torah so I can overhear a Jewish reading of the text.
>
> Then I talk about the text with someone, preferably a group of parishioners who discuss the lections on a weekly basis. Since the freshest comments often come from those who describe themselves as the least religious people, I make and keep friends outside the church who are willing to talk about sermons with me.
>
> —Barbara Brown Taylor

> In the broadest sense, preparation *for* the sermon includes all of our learning and life experiences. More specifically, it focuses on basic, background study of the text and theme.
>
> This is what I call the jotting stage of sermon preparation that begins at least several weeks, and often several months, before the Sunday on which it is to be preached.
>
> —Lowell Erdahl

Consultation of biblical commentaries can be the equivalent of sitting in thoughtful conversation with a wise friend about a biblical text.

> To begin to prepare a sermon without consulting at least one current commentary on the text is like doing a high dive into the shallow end of a pool. I don't have to agree with the commentator, and I have no intention of quoting the commentator, but I am grateful for the scholarly exploration of the text, for new insights and sometimes for the correction of long-held misunderstandings.
> —John Vannorsdall

Having been engaged by the text in a variety of ways, how do illustrations come to mind? It is important to keep an open mind at this point. Brainstorm, jot down images, stories, ideas as they come to mind. They can be organized and sifted later. Remember that we are seeking material that will help our hearers connect with a text. First impressions, immediate connections, are important.

Trusting Our Own Experience

Trust your own experience, particularly those experiences that specifically relate to the exact cultural location of your congregation.

> I find that the best supportive material for my sermons is the memories of my own life experiences, especially in my Dad's grocery store. The barrio philosophy and theology of our people was superb. The wisdom of the *viejitos* (beloved elderly) far surpasses anything else I have ever learned in theology or Bible classes. They probably had never read the Bible or studied the catechism, but they knew God quite well and communicated with him regularly. I have never gathered any supportive material for my sermons, however I have always maintained my studies in both the Bible and the human sciences.

Furthermore, the best supportive material seems to be the stories I pick up by just listening to the people—whether they come for counseling or I just meet them on the street—and reflections on my own life journey. Some of my conversations with prostitutes have given me some of my deepest and most moving testimonies about human nature. I can see why Jesus was so close to them and why he often said they would be the first into the kingdom. Some of my best sermon stories come from pastoral experiences. I do not like canned stories, I think my own life experiences are more credible, especially when I am willing to share honestly about my own failures, weaknesses, and stupidities.

—Virgilio Elizondo

Reading as a Source for Illustrations

Reading widely, aimlessly, and expectantly is an essential prerequisite for the collection of good illustrative material.

When I began reviewing non-fiction books for a local newspaper, I was assigned books on topics that I would not normally choose: auto racing, General Motors, mountain climbing, mining, canoeing. This was a happy eventuality.

For one, it gave me insights into all kinds of unfamiliar subjects and gave me more things to talk about with others.

For another, I came across all kinds of unexpected stories that served as excellent illustrations. (I loathe pious illustrations that are predictable and clichéd.)

—Arthur P. Boers

I am continually on the outlook for sermon material. I cannot imagine preaching on a regular basis without also reading on a regular basis. I always have a work of fiction, a book of poetry, and a book of theology going.

I read newspapers and *The New Yorker* religiously. I have found over the years that if I intend to be creative, I will need to surround myself with the thoughts of others who are also creative. It is not that their thoughts become my own; rather, their creativity brings my own creativity to life.

—Joanna Adams

Pastoral Ministry as a Source for Illustration

Reading is not the only source of vital illustration. The pastor's life, the pastor's daily interaction with the congregation is also a great source:

- Set aside observation times in different places each week (playground, lunch counter, park, hospital waiting room, sale barn, mall); look and write down what you see.
- Read pieces like "Hers" and "About Men" in the *New York Times Magazine* to get insights on men and women.
- Write inside back cover of books noting topics and page numbers to remember.
- I keep file folders of print pieces by topic (for example, downsizing) and some according to authors (for example, Quindlen, before she quit her column).
- Take a small notepad everywhere and use it to remember what you see and hear.

—Barbara Lundblad

A preacher is always on the prowl for apt illustration. The task is made easier by planning our preaching far enough in advance so that, with future texts and sermons in the back of our minds, we are ready to pounce on the apt illustration when we meet it.

Recording Illustrations

As we read and observe, we must also be prepared to record our insights and ideas.

For years, I have kept both topical files and files organized by authors/theologians. For example, the categories under the letter "D" are: David, Death, Dying and Christian Ethics,

Death Penalty, Demons, Denominations, Discipleship, Diversity, and Doubt. My author/theologian set of files begins with Maya Angelou and ends with Elie Wiesel. When I read, I make margin notations and mark the pages on which I have found quotable material. Afterwards, I will place a note in the appropriate file referencing that book.

—Joanna Adams

When I read books, I keep a slip of paper in my book. On it I note pages with quotes, subjects, or stories worth remembering. I file these references in one of three ways. I have binders with alphabetically arranged pages on a variety of topics. I include quotes, short illustrations, or references there. (For example, I have a list of references where to read about various theories and understandings of the atonement.) Some topics (prayer, forgiveness, Christology) are too large for a page or two in a binder and merit a file in my filing cabinet. I also make notes directly in my study Bible: interpretations (especially of difficult passages), references to where passages are explained, pithy quotes, and suggestions about illustrations.

—Arthur P. Boers

Current computer technology makes much of this laborious process unnecessary; with it we can easily cross reference our notes. After loading sermon illustrations and stories, a good word search program enables us to find a given illustration immediately by searching for one keyword. Thus is solved one of the preacher's greatest challenges—finding an illustration you need once you have saved it.

THINGS ENCOURAGED AND DISCOURAGED

Things Encouraged

- Read and listen widely.
- Become attentive to the conversations of others and the ways in which your people illustrate their own truths.
- Develop some systematic means of recording and retrieving illustrative material.
- Find your own voice, your own way of illustrating biblical truths from within your own experience.

Things Discouraged

- Don't trust your memory to recall an illustration, story, image, or conversation. Write it down!
- Avoid books of canned stories and illustrations.
- Use the illustrations of great preachers with care. If an illustration is very good, it has probably been overused.
- Take care in sharing the personal experiences of others; you must not betray a confidence in the pulpit.
- Never tell another person's experience as if it happened to you.
- Do not represent as true any story that is not true.

BEST ANSWERS TO QUESTIONS

- Must I write down potential illustrations?

    I keep a journal and record in detail observations, events, conversations, and even scenes while traveling. Names, dates, and places are recorded. And all this is in advance of and unrelated to any sermon. Reading through the journal, like reading through the Scriptures, enlarges one's sympathies, capacities, and understanding. And then on the occasion of preparing a sermon, something from the journal will urge itself into the message, and one will enter the pulpit with what is one's own, by this time well-fermented in the compost of the mind.

—Fred Craddock

I fill spiral notebooks (about a page a day) with ideas and phrases that I'll probably use in prayers, sermons, speeches. I read the *New York Times* daily, especially the editorials. I read *The Nation* and *The New Yorker* with some regularity, and constantly depend on experts to inform me about issues such as disarmament, economic justice, sexism, and homophobia. If these experts are in the congregation, so much the better.

—William Sloane Coffin

I make a habit to write down everything I see or hear that has the potential of enlightening a sermon. I do this because I can easily forget things unless I give them a more permanent form by writing them down. I have a "truth box" on my study desk where I put everything that I believe at the time might have potential for further use. I will periodically go through these and discover that many of the things have lost their life from the time I wrote them until the present. But unless I husband all of the possibilities, I find myself often sending my bucket down a dry well.

—John R. Claypool

• Isn't there something to be said for purchasing books of illustrations from the great preachers of the past?

I do not recommend buying books of illustrations. Most of them are dated or overused if they are good stories. Quoting a Clarence McCartney story in my church does not even bring a twitch in the congregation. Often, it takes too much explanation of who the person is. By the time the preacher gets to the story, the listeners are exhausted.

I also avoid long, involved stories. People are conditioned too much by the immediacy of television to follow a long, convoluted story.

—Charles Bugg

• What about sharing stories that arise from my day-to-day pastoral experiences with my people? Isn't this getting too personal?

Listening to people in your congregation never means sharing their stories from the pulpit (even when you move to the next parish). Personal hurts (such as abuse, addiction, incest) can enter sermons through *public media stories* (a television special, a newspaper story, a movie). Breaking silence is an important part of preaching, but it never means breaking confidence.

—Barbara Lundblad

• Aside from reading and observing, are there other intentional, systematic ways in which I can develop my own ability to find and utilize illustrative material?

I am a member of several study groups, one of which I found particularly useful in recent years. It consists of ministers from several different denominations and works like this: Five to ten of us gather on Tuesday morning. Our convener reads the Psalm for the following Sunday, then we read the Sunday lectionary texts together. Each of us chooses one of the texts on which to meditate. The convener plays a tape of music, and we sit together, reflecting, praying, and writing for the next forty-five minutes. At the end of that time, those of us who wish to do so, share with one another our written reflections. It is incredible how strongly the Holy Spirit shows up, disclosing new insights to often familiar passages.

—Joanna Adams

CONCLUSION

We have thus found, in listening to the good advice of our preachers, that collecting supportive material for our sermons is more than a matter of technique—finding, collecting, recording, finding again—it is also a state of mind, a way of living in the world full of confidence that the Holy Spirit reveals truth to us through our experiences. The first step in good preaching is good listening. The cultivation of a fertile homiletical imagination is related to constant dialogue with the imaginations of others.

Robin Meyers gives us a useful benediction for this chapter:

> And remember that you can get lost in the voices of other people. Find your own voice, and never underestimate the power of what happens to you as a pastor every single day. Read the text aloud and roll key words around in your mouth before you go to the commentaries. Be playful and imaginative, and remember: until you've heard, nobody will be able to hear you.

BIBLIOGRAPHY

Cox, James W., "Illustrations," in William H. Willimon and Richard Lischer, *The Concise Encyclopedia of Preaching*. Louisville: Westminster/John Knox Press, 1995.

Long, Thomas G., "Images and Experiences in Sermons," in *The Witness of Preaching*. Louisville: Westminster/John Knox Press, 1989.

5
ORGANIZING MATERIAL
John S. McClure

An inexperienced preacher once asked a seasoned preacher how many points a sermon should have. Without pausing the preacher answered, "At least one!" Unless hearers know what preachers are talking about, they will never be able to understand and respond to their messages. For this reason, preachers should give ample attention to organizing their materials—message, theology, Scripture, and illustration—before they preach.

> After preparing *for* the sermon and filling several pages with disordered jottings, emphasis shifts from preparation *for* to preparation *of* the sermon. Preparation *of* the sermon centers on the selection and the ordering of thought.
> —Lowell Erdahl

At this point in sermon preparation, the preacher decides *what* to say and *how* to say it.

> I have found Fred Craddock's insight to be very helpful when it comes to shaping one's material for a sermon. He says there must be two eureka moments for the preacher to create one eureka moment for the listener. The first moment is deciding what you want to say in terms of a central theme, the second is deciding how to package this

so it will be understood and connect with all the faculties of the listener.

—John R. Claypool

GOALS

• Preach a significant message with a significant purpose.
The first goal of organization is to preach a message that is worth preaching. It is easy to engage in exegesis and sermon brainstorming week after week and arrive at themes that lack both significance and relevance. A good way to decide whether a theme is worth preaching is to ask whether it generates passion in our own hearts.

> If I'm not stirred by the message I write, I can't expect anyone else to be stirred by the message.
> —April Larson

> I do not think that we should preach if we do not have something to say, something we truly feel passionate about. Passion should be the basis of preaching so that it can lead the congregation to an experience of the presence of God in their midst. It should not be just information—our task is to proclaim.
> —Virgilio Elizondo

Without a significant purpose, a sermon theme is likely to fall flat in the pulpit. The preacher can ask whether a theme speaks a needed and important word to the gathered congregation. Does this message bring hope? Offer comfort or encouragement? Challenge? Impart vision?

What difference does this witness make for those who will hear the sermon?

—John Vannorsdall

• Be clear and maintain interest.

Having decided upon a significant message, the preacher's second goal is to preach this message in a way that is clear and will maintain the hearer's interest. Clarity is usually a function of the logical arrangement of material and the careful use of transitions. We need to reveal enough of our sermon structure to let hearers know where we are in the process of conveying our thought.

> As a parish minister, I have moved to letting more of the structure show in the sermon. I'm convinced that many folks who come to church are overwhelmed, tired, and hardly able to listen to a sermon that has no cohesiveness, no direction and is too full of ambiguity.
>
> —Charles Bugg

Hearers need to know that they are onboard a vehicle that has a pilot who is not lost, but has a road map and the skills necessary to navigate the highway and terrain ahead.

> Sermons are a trip, not just a destination, and what matters to the listener is that all of us are going somewhere together.
>
> —Robin Meyers

INSTRUCTIONS

The Emerging Theme

In some instances preachers organize their material intuitively, allowing the sermon's theme and form to emerge out of the bits and pieces of the brainstorming process.

> What I do is this: I jot down ideas, possible sermon trajectories, potential sermon illustrations, in no particular order or importance. For resources, I look to my current reading, my files, experiences in the life of the parish, experiences in my own life, among other things. The next day, I go over my notes to see if I can discern any emerging themes or patterns. I am often surprised at what emerges, and I have learned over the years to trust my instincts. When I begin to write, I usually have a clear idea of where the sermon is going, but now and then, I am genuinely surprised. The two constants in the process are the awareness that I need to have my destination in mind and a commitment to take the congregation with me. Nothing is worse than a sermon that meanders. I try to bring it home each week.
> —Joanna Adams

> Sometimes I need to start writing first in order to put on paper what *I should not say.* Writing it down allows that unhelpful voice to be named and seen for what it is and set aside. Writing helps me sort.
> —April Larson

According to our preachers, it is often the case that a sermon structure will spring forth after the preacher decides on a particular, unified idea or message to preach.

I find it helpful to write in the center of a sheet of paper my theme or focus sentence. This is the message, distilled and drawn from study of the text. As Luther said, "First the flower, then the meadow." Then I circle this statement with related material drawn from related texts, theological reflection, news reports, observations, experience, congregational life, history, biography, general reading, and so on. Lines are drawn from these sketched pieces (to be fleshed out later) to the central message, like spokes in a wheel. Any material that does not connect with the message, no matter how good it seems, is eliminated from this sermon, but saved for another time. Next, I list these items in no particular order and begin the process of arranging them as they will appear in the sermon. I usually arrange and re-arrange four or five times.

—Fred Craddock

• Meditate and mull over the readings until a basic idea takes hold.
• Write, type, dictate everything that comes to mind on that subject.
• Organize the material under several headings or points.
• Begin serious writing on each of these points (not necessarily finishing each point before going on to the next).

—Walter Burghardt

As the preacher meditates on a central theme, two questions will help produce a discernable pattern of thought for the sermon: What divisions of thought are inherent in this larger theme? How can I build my sermon so my hearers and I will arrive at this complete thought by the end of the sermon?

The Sermon of Purpose

Another way to discover a form for the sermon is to focus attention on the purpose of the sermon, rather than on its theme.

What shape seems best suited to this focus? Where do I hope to go with the listeners today? If I want them to see God's promises (even when there seems little evidence), can I help them see Isaiah's image of the shoot growing from a stump? This sermon will lift up this image—What is this image like in my life, your life? Where have I seen this in my neighborhood? Every sermon needs to be organized and preached with our partners/listeners in mind.

—Barbara Lundblad

The Logic of the Text

Some preachers find it helpful to ask if there is a shape or form of logic in the biblical text that can be transposed into a sermonic form.

Often the form of the biblical story will determine how material is organized. Some texts lend themselves to narrative preaching, others to a more argument-oriented form.

—James Henry Harris

I think my best sermons have followed closely a biblical text, which structures the sermon and keeps me biblical.

—William Sloane Coffin

I encourage preachers to be guided by the form of the Scripture itself. Scripture offers at least the following shapes: visual images, narratives, parables, letters, prayers, songs, conversations, laments, teachings, oracles, visions, and more.

—Barbara Lundblad

Deductive and Inductive Sermons

In general, there are two primary ways that sermons can be organized: deductively and inductively. The deductive sermon moves from the presentation of a general truth to its application or illustrative support. The preacher presents his or her conclusions and then supports these conclusions in various ways. The deductive outline looks like this:

I.
  A.
    1.
      a.
      b.
II.

As Fred Craddock demonstrated in his classic book, *As One without Authority*, the inductive sermon moves from the presentation of the particulars of experience toward a general truth. According to Craddock, the hearer is invited to arrive at conclusions similar to those of the preacher by traveling on a similar journey toward those conclusions. The inductive outline might look like this:

      a.
      b.
    1.
  A.
I.

Deductive preachers and hearers are not as happy with ambiguity and the process of discovery in preaching. They feel that it is important to present what is being talked about quickly and clearly. The flow of meaning and ideas is arrested at each point along the way, and hearers are told continually what it is that the preacher is talking about—idea, point, message.

> Browne Barr taught me to have a lively introduction, basically to make three points and to conclude. For me, the format has worked pretty well.
> —William Sloane Coffin

Inductive preachers and hearers enjoy more ambiguity and delay in the arrival of final meanings and conclusions. What the preacher is talking about is detoured as the hearer participates in a set of shared experiences that lead up to the preacher's point.

> Inductive preaching facilitates the most essential ingredient in persuasion: participation. Telling someone something new is not as important as helping them to recognize the truth of something they already know.
> —Robin Meyers

Sometimes, inductive sermons are left open-ended to invite the listener to supply the conclusion.

> I almost never draw conclusions at the end of a sermon. I may put all the pieces of the puzzle out on the table, but I won't make everyone watch while I put it together. At the very least, I want my listeners to have to pleasure of popping in the last piece for themselves.
> —Barbara Brown Taylor

Plotted Sermons

> I believe the qualities of a good story should also be the qualities of a good sermon. Jesus utilized the element of surprise. I have found that sermons that take an unexpected turn make the deepest impressions.
> —John R. Claypool

Eugene Lowry, in *The Homiletical Plot*, shows how sermons can be arranged like the plot of a good novel, drama, or short story. The plotted sermon begins with a sense of uneasy equilibrium that includes some foreshadowing of potential problems. Then, this equilibrium is upset as an enigma is presented that energizes the sermon's forward movement. Something is wrong that needs fixing; something is out of balance that needs restoration; something is missing that needs to be found; something is confusing that needs clarification. The body of the sermon is spent delaying the restoration of equilibrium. This delay is accomplished by either deepening the enigma or by snaring the hearer into considering potential, partial, or unsatisfactory resolutions. The gospel then provides a significant clue or twist in the plot that leads to a restoration of equilibrium.

Conversational Sermons

Another form of logic that preachers and homileticians are only just beginning to understand and employ intentionally is the logic of conversation. Instead of moving from or toward conclusions or resolutions, a conversation gives the sense of a back and forth, dialogical movement in pursuit of a shared meaning. To discover this natural, conversational sermon form, it is helpful to hold a roundtable conversation with a group of laity about the biblical preaching text prior to organizing the sermon material. The dynamics of this conversation can become the actual dynamics of the sermon preached. Keeping the image of the sermon as a roundtable conversation in the forefront of the mind during sermon preparation helps the preacher to organize the sermon conversationally. Several things are notable about conversational speech.

• Qualifiers.
The preacher will tend to use more qualifiers: "It seems that," "Could it be that," "Maybe. . . ."

• Following.
The preacher will acknowledge, from time to time, that the sermon is following the hearer's lead in pursuing a topic of conversation. "Some of you have expressed concern. . . ." "In response to. . . ."

• Repair.
The preacher will revise (repair) his or her ideas in light of new information provided by the hearers or by the biblical text. "Until recently I thought that . . . but after . . . I've decided. . . ."

• Linking and differing.
The preacher will link or differentiate his or her ideas with those of the hearers. "You and I see this in several different ways. . . ."

• Frame resistance and reframing.
The preacher will sometimes resist dominant frames in order to
include others at the roundtable. "Let's see if there are other ways
to look at this. . . ." At other times, the preacher will show how
new insights emerge if the hearer reframes a topic from another
perspective. "There's a connection here that you and I may never
have considered if it weren't for those who have experienced. . . ."

• Empathic response.
The preacher will sometimes paraphrase potential feelings about a
thought. (Qualifiers will help the preacher avoid imputing feelings
that do not exist.) "Some of us may feel the need for. . . ."

These and many other conversational dynamics yield a recipro-
cating form of logic that moves the sermon along toward a variety
of shared meanings and applications for the hearers.

Stock Patterns

Preachers can use a variety of stock pattern. These can be found in
books on public speaking and basic homiletics textbooks (see Bibliography below). Stock patterns include:

• Time patterns.
Ideas are distributed according to chronological time: first, second,
third, and so on. Another chronological pattern discusses the way
things are now and then goes back to speak about how things were
during earlier stages or periods.

• Space patterns.
Sometimes ideas lend themselves to spatial organization: "On
one side," "on the other side," and "in the middle." Another spatial pattern locates ideas geographically: "In Jerusalem," and "In
Ephesus. . . ."

• Conditional patterns.
Ideas build on each other in an if-then pattern. "If this . . . then this
. . . and this. . . ."

• Faceting patterns.

The subject is treated like a diamond held up and turned slowly in order to examine all of its facets.

• Problem-solution patterns.

The preacher analyzes a problem and proposes or explains a solution.

Introductions and Conclusions

> However it is done, the beginning and ending of a sermon are especially important, like the take-off and landing of an airplane. Find a way to capture the congregation's attention immediately and at the ending to draw things together.
> —J. Philip Wogaman

> I am not one for formal introductions and conclusions. I do not, as the old advice goes, say what I'm going to say, say it, then say what I said. I like people to pay attention and I'm willing to make them work at it, hoping that I reward their work with something worthwhile.
> —Arthur P. Boers

Although introductions and conclusions are not used with all forms of preaching or by all preachers, there is always the need for careful attention to the way that sermons are begun and ended. The beginning of a sermon should not only capture the attention of the hearer, it should relate the subject matter of the sermon immediately to significant human issues or concerns.

> I believe that the purpose of the introduction is not just to introduce the theme and lead into the message of the text, but especially to indicate that this sermon intends to do some vital business with the listener. We can capture attention by being humorous or dramatic but it is far better to gain and hold attention by starting with something that prompts the hearer to think, "This sounds important to me."
> —Lowell Erdahl

The beginning of a sermon should be designed to get listeners on board the sermonic vehicle. The only way to do this is to make sure that listeners know that the vehicle is going somewhere that they need to go. This does not mean that preachers provide a complete outline of the sermon. This can destroy the spirit of suspense and open-endedness that is so vital to maintaining interest. Rather, it means that the hearer is given a clear sense of the thematic horizon into which they are traveling. Hearers must be oriented to the sermon's subject matter. Sometimes this is done deductively, by directly stating the sermon's theme and suggesting its significance for the listener. Other times it is done inductively, by way of story, metaphor, or image.

> I do generally like to introduce the theme with a story or an extended metaphor or reflection on a life situation that catches people's attention and piques their interest. I often prefer to do this in a way that catches people off guard. I do not like pious and predictable stories, but prefer to keep people guessing for a bit: "Where is this going?" "Why are we being told this odd story?" From this story, metaphor, or image, I like to back into the theme of the sermon or an aspect of the sermon's theme, gradually easing people into the connection.
>
> —Arthur P. Boers

Introductions not only orient the hearer to the entire sermon, but they clearly connect the hearer to the first movement of thought in the sermon itself. The same is true of conclusions. Good conclusions grow naturally out of the final movement of thought in a sermon. They also complete the thought of the entire sermon.

The goal of a conclusion is to bring all of the ideas that have been covered in the sermon into one single focus. The way that this is done is dependent upon the purpose of the sermon as a whole. If the purpose was to persuade or to teach, then the conclusion might recapitulate the main argument or objective of the sermon. If the purpose was to inspire, then the sermon may end with a story or a challenge. If the purpose was to convict or to convince, then the preacher might ask for a decision or for renewed commitment.

THINGS ENCOURAGED AND DISCOURAGED

Things Encouraged

• Start early.

To give sufficient attention to organizing the sermon, the preacher needs to begin the process of sermon preparation early in the week.

> I think that it is very important to get at the shaping of the sermon as early as possible. It would terrify me to simply wait until Saturday to prepare for Sunday morning!
> —J. Philip Wogaman

• Know what to leave out.

> Another thing about organizing the material is the wisdom involved in what to leave out. Here is where the preacher's ego can become an obstacle, for we are tempted to put things in a sermon so that people will be dazzled by the breadth of our reading or the depth of our insight when, in fact, the goal of preaching is to glorify God and make the hearer amazed in relation to that Mystery. Whatever illustrations are used should be inherent to the central thrust of that particular sermon. One of the tests of the maturity of a preacher is to hear a really good story on Friday and not use it in Sunday's sermon. Remember that parish ministers have many chances to teach and illumine their congregations. They do not have to do it all in a single presentation.
> —John R. Claypool

• Use clear transitions.

Transitions include such common terms as *and, in addition, but, yet, perhaps, so, because, despite this, not only . . . but also, if . . .*

then, besides, on the other hand, another way to see . . ., the third . . ., and another. These and other similar words can be used in conjunction with transitional sentences to provide closure for one thought, show how the next thought is related to the one being left behind, and suggest something of the content of the upcoming portion of the sermon. Transitions are needed to let the hearer know that they are on the right path, moving in the right direction. Without transitions, hearers are left floundering, with no signposts to guide them in their hearing.

> Please tell me where you are going in this sermon. I have no idea how you got from a boat on the Sea of Galilee to peanuts on a flight to Cleveland. You know what you are doing, I presume, but I need the help of transitions that allow me to review where we have been and where we are going.
>   —John Vannorsdall

• Know when to conclude.
Nothing is more bothersome than a sermon that rambles on and on. Good preachers learn when they have exhausted the development of their message and move quickly to conclude. Words such as *finally* or *in conclusion* should be avoided unless the preacher is actually planning to conclude.

• Vary the tone.
Different homiletical purposes require different tones of voice and moods in the pulpit. Varying one's tone will harmonize the sermon with the preacher's purpose and overcome the tedium of monotonous (monotonal) preaching.

> Very early on in the production of a sermon we should have made a decision about the nature of the sermon: What will the tone be—argumentative? declarative? slightly poetic? meditative? reminiscent? solemn? light-hearted? There is a danger of becoming addicted to one particular tone too early in a preaching career that can lead to boredom in the pew.
>   —David H. C. Read

• Vary the form.

As the preacher becomes more advanced and aware of the many possibilities for organizing material, it is important to work to master several ways to preach sermons. To expand one's repertoire of sermon forms, the preacher can first consider which sermon forms are used most naturally. The preacher can look back over past sermons and try to determine what patterns are most commonly used.

> After fifty-five years of preaching, I am more than ever convinced that, where sermon form is the issue, there are no absolutes, there is not just one form to be imposed on all. The criterion I advise is: Within what form(s) is this preacher most comfortable and most effective? I myself am more comfortable, more effective, with the deductive sermon form, perhaps from my long-term immersion in Scholastic philosophy and theology, but I recognize the advantages of other forms, and have experienced their effectiveness in other preachers.
> —Walter Burghardt

Having determined one's native gifts, and realizing that everyone cannot shape sermons after the manner of Fred Craddock or Frederick Buechner, the preacher can move on to learn other ways of communicating that will enhance their preaching.

> I believe that we ministers need to develop as full a range of homiletical muscles as we can. We need to develop our own repertoire.
> —Charles Bugg

• Negotiate a hearing for new forms of preaching.

Preachers should be attentive to the expectations that already exist in the congregation. If a congregation has grown accustomed to hearing deductive, three-points-and-a-prayer preaching, the preacher needs to move slowly to negotiate a hearing for narrative or inductive models.

A great deal of how a preacher shapes material depends
on how a congregation listens, as well as that minister's
own gifts.

—Charles Bugg

Things Discouraged

• Don't over-organize.

It is important to keep these organizational tools in perspective.
They exist as homiletical servants, not as ends in and of themselves. Preachers should be careful not to let slavery to form deter
them from doing what is necessary in the moment of delivery to
communicate the Word of God.

I think we take the passion out of preaching when we try to
over-organize it. Our task is to proclaim, not to control the
action of grace—we must leave that to the Spirit.

—Virgilio Elizondo

• Don't use show-off forms.

When our sermon forms become too visible, sermons become gim-
micky and self-serving. I once heard an Easter sermon using the
acronym RESURRECTION as an organizational tool. Like a cheer-
leader, the preacher shouted: "R is for . . ., E is for . . ., S is for. . . ."
The result was silly and distracting.

• Avoid long-winded introductions and conclusions.

In some circles it has become fashionable to do what amounts to
sermon set-ups. Preachers engage in lengthy pre-sermon explanations of the texts, recapitulations of exegesis, contextualizations,
or apologetics. Sometimes these set-ups are placed at the beginning of the sermon itself as long introductions. At other times the
introduction becomes a lengthy digression during which the
preacher rambles around, deciding out loud what to talk about.
Most homiletics professors testify that they can often flip two or
three pages into a sermon manuscript and find the true beginning
point of the sermon. When too much time is spent introducing

one's material, preachers run out of time. If the preacher worries that, "I don't have time to develop my last point," it is a good idea to go back and see if the introduction is not too long. To maintain a sense of immediacy, keep the attention of hearers, and have time to deepen and round out our messages, it is crucial that introductory material be focused and limited.

> It's too common for us to spend most of our preparation time on set-em-up stories and a re-statement of the text. Since we have by then run out of preparation time, the sermon concludes with clichés about how God loves us/saves us/frees us, and we never get to images of what these things mean for the various rages and dilemmas in our hearts.
> —John Vannorsdall

Likewise, conclusions should be brief. Nothing is worse than constantly concluding conclusions. Keep in mind that new material should never be introduced in a conclusion.

> When listening to a sermon, I try to remember how often I have wondered, "Why did she or he not stop right there?" And how seldom I have thought, "Please go on."
> —David H. C. Read

BEST ANSWERS TO QUESTIONS

• What about using outlines?

Our preachers are divided on the use of outlines. Some use various kinds of outlines. Others draw lines and arrows. Several begin writing immediately and then go back to organize or sort. With my students, I sometimes use a sermon-sequencing grid that moves from left to right to help them organize their material.

Table 1	Sequence 1	Sequence 2	Sequence 3	Sequence 4
Theology				
Message				
Illustration				
Scripture				

Essentially, preachers must determine for themselves what works best. The main thing is to remember to do some careful organizational work before preaching.

• What about mixing sermon forms?

> Personally, I have tried to blend several components into each sermon. I will have some deductive moments into which I weave stories or use inductive methods such as questions. I question whether a preacher has to begin the preparation of a sermon by choosing one form over all others. Why not use different communicative forms in the same sermon?
>
> —Charles Bugg

Sometimes it is possible to mix two or three forms together. Be careful, however, not to create hybrid forms that are so complex that they cannot be followed by your hearers.

• What about making applications?

In an earlier day, preachers were told to always end sermons with applications. This meant that hearers were given something to do. If action is the desired result of a sermon, then applications are appropriate. Preachers should remember to include themselves in such directives.

> I'm all for giving them something to do, but that should include me, too. Example is still the best form of teaching.
> —William Sloane Coffin

Too much application, however, sometimes seems to intrude on the work of the Holy Spirit in preaching.

> I personally do not like to give them something to do. I would rather try to proclaim the word of God and leave the response to each one of them. I should not try to manipulate the action of Grace. If it has been a true sermon, they, illuminated by grace, will think of what to do—it may not be something I would think of, or maybe even approve of, but I need to trust the action of the Spirit.
> —Virgilio Elizondo

Specific forms of action may not be the desired result of every sermon. Applications should be used primarily when action or behavior are the preacher's goals.

CONCLUSION

Crafting a sermon begins with discerning a significant gospel message and discovering the right form to communicate that message to a particular congregation. Paying attention to the organization of sermonic materials (message, theology, scripture, and illustration) leaves the preacher with the feeling of being on top of sermon preparation. The only way to develop organizational skills is to experiment with outlines, various sermon forms, introductions, conclusions, transitions, sermon purposes, and tones. The rewards of these exercises in experiential learning are worth the effort: sermons that make sense and stir the hearer's interest and commitment week after week.

BIBLIOGRAPHY

Craddock, Fred, *As One Without Authority*. Nashville: Abingdon Press, 1979.

DeVito, Joseph A. *Human Communication: The Basic Course*. New York: Harper and Row, Publishers, 4th edition, 1988.

Long, Thomas G., *The Witness of Preaching*. Louisville: Westminster/John Knox Press, 1989.

Lowry, Eugene, *The Homiletical Plot*. Atlanta: John Knox Press, 1980.

McClure, John S., *The Roundtable Pulpit*. Nashville: Abingdon Press, 1995.

6

POLISHING
THE SERMON

Henry H. Mitchell

The apparently natural, effortless performance of good preachers may make the subject of sermon polishing seem strange and superfluous to many who hear them. Let it be clearly understood that the apparent ease of good preaching is precisely what every preacher should strive for. All of us should step out of the spotlight and let the hearers focus on the Word.

This idea of polishing may also be foreign to preachers who believe that God tells them directly what to say. God does indeed inspire messages, but God expects us to take the initial inspiration and give it our best development and refinement. God does not do for preachers what they could and should do for themselves. Even the special, concluding help of the Holy Spirit during delivery is reserved for preachers who can honestly cry, "Now Lord, I've done all I know to do, but if you don't improve it and speak through your servant, there'll be no preaching today."

The process of polishing the sermon is parallel to the task of sandpapering a fine piece of cabinet work. One carefully and painstakingly removes the less obvious irregularities from a given surface. The rough places aren't glaring at first sight, but they will put a run in a pair of nylon hose or even scratch the skin a little. In a word, the polishing of a sermon is the difference between a good job and a mediocre one. It is the critical factor between an optimal hearing and one unnecessarily disrupted by seemingly minor and easily correctable details.

These details have to do with things such as grammar, tense and person consistency, sentence and paragraph structure, transition, and precision. Polishing the sermon includes using proper word choice, pronunciation, and imagery and avoiding outworn language, clichés, colloquialisms, and slang. Another subtle but important detail involves preparing a sermon to be heard, as opposed to being read.

> In polishing the sermon, it should be remembered that preaching is an oral event and not a written essay. Therefore, we need to think constantly about how the sermon is going to sound to people who are listening rather than reading.
> —John R. Claypool

It is naïve to expect all these details to be cared for in the first flush of either inspiration or, as sometimes happens, desperation. The best advice I know of is to let the creativity gush forth profusely and without inhibition *first*. After that, do a second or third draft and deal with flow and content. Follow this with a careful final polishing.

GOALS

• Free the hearer to forget the preacher.
One does not enter the polishing process motivated by a desire to project an image of perfection or omnicompetence. The purpose is not to attract attention to the preacher as person or even as communicator. Rather, the goal is to avoid the waste of a good sermon for want of a few touch-ups that could smooth out the listening process and allow complete concentration on the heard word. One is not showcasing the speaker's brilliance, but freeing the hearer to forget the preacher completely and to see and hear the gospel.

• Encounter with God and Word.

By freeing the hearer to forget the preacher, we are preparing the way for an *experiential encounter with God and the Word*. The achievement of any such goal is dependent, of course, on the intended audience. They should be kept in the back of one's mind constantly.

> Throughout the writing process we must have in mind the intended audience (real people, believers, half-believers, and unbelievers), so that communication with them may be as direct as possible.
>
> —David H. C. Read

It is all too often the case, however, that we preachers concentrate more on our own response to the proposed Word. Thus the need, near the end of the process, to polish the work by fully sitting where the audience sits and listening for how *they* are likely to understand and identify with what we intend to say. Our goal is to address the whole personhood of the hearer (rational, intuitive, and emotive consciousness) so that the word is retained in unforgettable images and experiences.

This may be a fresh, even strange insight for many. Let me explain: We all want to preach a moving sermon, but our preparation often yields an intellectually impressive sermon—an essay, to be brutally blunt. We leave the moving part to the Holy Spirit. Now, to be sure, there is a great wisdom here, but where our writing is, there will our sermons be also. Our true goal is evidenced in the mode of our writing, and that's the goal the Holy Spirit will honor, no matter how much we *say* we wish to have a stirring impact.

The shift to a holistic encounter with God and the Word may require a major effort if we are to overcome a cultural bias against including emotive involvement. We may have to engage in exercises focusing on the worthiness of both the intellectual *and* behavioral goals of preaching. Feelings are important if we are to inspire behavior. Jesus himself said many times that the bottom line was in the doing.

It will help greatly to read good literature and become aware of the ways great writers succeed in moving us.

I urge the preacher to move away from the work on the sermon and read good literature—stories and poetry by people who write extremely well. Why? Because many of the resources we use in study are valued for their content, but scholar/authors may not be good writers. Therefore, the need now is to place oneself among good communicators, people who know how to present a character, describe a scene, follow an event, or create an effect.

—Fred Craddock

The Bible itself is often as moving as it is because of vivid, gripping, and moving descriptions. We are as moved by a vivid word picture as the centurion in Matthew 27:54 was moved by the real scene. Seeing the actual crucifixion, he risked his lifetime career and burst forth with, "Truly this was the Son of God." We can see it through words.

I can say this because a high school camp's vesper preacher with this same story moved the whole camp, including me, just that much. Although it was nearly fifty years ago, I can still visualize details like the centurion's hobnailed boots and leather girdle. I can *see* this tough top sergeant in the Roman army trying to hold back his tears and his costly words. And I will never forget the effect of that mountaintop message on 110 campers, their counselors, and me.

This vesper preacher was a former college president. He was quite familiar with the abstractions so important in seminaries. But his seemingly effortless ad lib picture message, which was delivered in near darkness on a rugged point overlooking a valley, had been skillfully polished. His grammar and diction were superb, but I wasn't aware of this at the time. I saw it later in 20/20 hindsight. We turn now to what he must have done to help us see our Lord and that centurion so clearly and powerfully.

INSTRUCTIONS

Grammar and Consistency

Polish the grammar first. Use subjects, verbs, and possessives properly. Be consistent in narrative time and editorial perspective. Ask: Am I speaking in the past, present, or future tense? Am I telling a story as an observer or participant (first-person perspective), or as one without personal involvement (third-person perspective)? Scan the text for inconsistencies, then read it aloud to hear flaws not seen with the eye.

> Often it is not until I deliver a sermon out loud that I find crucial or structural flaws that need work or rearranging. Also, during this time, I sometimes underscore words or phrases that I want to stress and emphasize.
> —Arthur P. Boers

Once grammar and consistency have been dealt with, put them out of conscious concern. Mistakes in these details may disrupt the hearing of thoughtful hearers, and this should be avoided if possible. However, hearers will lose even more if these concerns override the desire to be used by the Holy Spirit in communicating biblical relevance and power.

Sentence Structure

> I try to guard against long, convoluted sentences.
> —Joanna Adams

Most of us struggle with the perennial problem of sentence structure. In the first draft of this chapter, some of my sentences took more than four typewritten lines. I know quite well that more than two-and-a-half lines per sentence makes problems for the ear. Be sure that sentences have clear subjects and predicates and that they are not too long.

Paragraph Structure

Possibly the greatest sin of the American pulpit is the long and unfocused paragraph. Long paragraphs aren't as obvious to the ear as to the eye, but they can destroy good flow as well as the hearer's ability to follow. A good paragraph has a topic sentence, a few sentences that explain the topic, followed by a closing summary sentence. Paragraphs longer than this will be out of balance and cover too many topics.

The only other element in a paragraph may be a transitional word or phrase that leads to the next paragraph or idea. Checking for transitions often has to await the final polish, because rushes of great inspiration seem not to care much about such things. Remember that our hearers have only one crack at the sermon. They can easily be put in the predicament of wondering how we got from one point to another.

> I pay particular attention to the transitions of the sermon. Does the sermon have logical movement, and does it progress smoothly from one thing to another?
> —Charles Bugg

Words

• Choose the right words and choose them well.

> While composing a sermon, let the preacher have a good dictionary at his or her elbow. Why? To assure that a word actually means what the preacher thinks it means or says what he or she wants to say.
> —Walter Burghardt

• Sometimes a definition is needed.

The hearer may not have understood a particular point or statement; therefore, the preacher offers spontaneous and synonymous statements or phrases to bring clarity to what was initially said.

—James Henry Harris

• Use clear nouns and verbs. Add adjectives and adverbs sparingly.

Be as precise as possible with verbs and nouns, avoid piles of adverbs and adjectives. "Shuffled" works better than "walked slowly."

—Barbara Lundblad

Particularity

Particularity carries more power and meaning than universality: err on the side of particularity even if it feels like leaving some people out.

—Barbara Lundblad

The power of particularity is the result of clear imagery and concrete detail that lead to the possibility of personal identification. The hearer is drawn into what is being said. The scriptural story becomes her or his story, and choices for action are made from within this in-depth identification.

Particularity is the key to an experiential encounter with God in preaching. Polishing for particularity is no mere literary nicety; it is the effort to be sure that listeners, by the power of the Holy Spirit, will be led not only to know but actually to do the very will of God.

Pronunciation

Polishing includes deciding how to pronounce difficult words. The meaning of words is lost when the hearer hears an obvious mispronunciation. Identification of biblical persons and places is likewise rendered impossible by a preacher's heroic stab at a proper name. We preachers owe it to the audience to find out ahead of time how to pronounce words that we are not sure about.

Polishing for proper pronunciation is also essential to credibility. Mispronunciation suggests that the preacher is using unfamiliar or non-original material. This is especially true of words of three or more syllables. If a word cannot be pronounced properly and with ease, don't use it. Polish it out.

Delivery

One aspect of polishing that can't be accomplished in the pastor's study is delivery. The best grammar, words, pronunciation, and idiom can be wasted when the preacher's chin is buried in his or her chest or his or her voice is muffled or distorted.

> Audibility is the most basic ingredient of effective preaching and one that is often sadly forgotten by many beginning preachers who keep their heads buried in their notes, their voices at a conversational pitch, and their microphones turned down low.
>
> —Joanna Adams

The next chapter will treat delivery in some depth. Here I only want to emphasize that delivery can be polished in the same way that we polish sermon content. Before preaching, practice naturally and firmly projecting the voice so that all may hear. This requires good support from the diaphragm. It also requires cultivating confidence—letting go of shyness or subtle withdrawal from the audience.

THINGS ENCOURAGED AND DISCOURAGED

Things Encouraged

• Expand your vocabulary.

The purpose of expanding our vocabularies is to use a wider variety of the words everybody knows, instead of using unfamiliar and esoteric expressions.

> The preacher needs to check out synonyms that are more imaginative, vivid, picturesque, that give color to our abstractions; to increase the preacher's vocabulary, so as not to bog down in a predictable diction that cannot possibly fire or inspire.
>
> —Walter J. Burghardt

• Refine, refine, refine.

> I continue this process of refining right up to the moment when I give the sermon.
>
> —John R. Claypool

• Use the language of the heart.

Proper language needs to become a habit, but proper is not the same in every speech community. Whatever the language, one needs to speak directly from the heart.

> The language of the gospel, and therefore the language of my preaching, is the ordinary language of the street and marketplace—this is incarnational language. I think that the language of preaching should be the language of the heart so that we might communicate heart to heart rather than head to head.
>
> —Virgilio Elizondo

Things Discouraged

• Don't use unnecessary words.
Avoid saying in ten words what can be said in four.

> Let the preacher go carefully over his text, expunge unnecessary words, phrases, sentences, perhaps paragraphs; make sure that the sermon is constantly moving, going somewhere, not stalled or encumbered in thought or language.
> —Walter J. Burghardt

Related to this is the unfortunate fascination some preachers have with listening to their own voices. The excess words are only vehicles for the resonant projection of their presumably pleasant and magnetic vocal tones. The cure is relatively easy if one is scanning a manuscript. The greater problem, however, is with those who use outlines or no notes. One helpful self-discipline consists of suffering through hearing one's own sermon played back on a tape recorder, with a view to spotting wordiness. This exercise has good potential for motivating one to more economy with words.

• Avoid excessive negativity.
It is so much easier to criticize than to be creatively constructive and to give thoughtful solutions. Like bulldozers in the construction business, one can wax spectacular in demolition, tearing down in three weeks what took three years to build. The only trouble is that there is no building of any kind left on the lot when one is finished.

I advise the preacher to make sure that the anatomy of sin (if indeed there is need for it) is no more than a third of the sermon. This third should neither start nor end the sermon. Opening with the whip loses the attention of the audience. The closing third needs to be devoted to empowerment of the hearers and celebration that motivates.

Never scold. Pour contempt, yes, but never scold. The prophets didn't!
—William Sloane Coffin

BEST ANSWERS TO QUESTIONS

• Should I add humor to my sermons?
One of the most frequent queries encountered in classes has to do with the use of humor in sermons. The use of jokes as warm-ups at the outset of a sermon is to me a cheap move for attention. If there is to be humor, let it be a legitimate part of the gospel.

> About humor, my own rule is let it come as a natural response to some situation or turn of speech, but don't drag it in just because it's Easter morning.
> —David H. C. Read

I would usually be quite reluctant to tell a joke, as such, anywhere in the sermon, unless it was a truly effective way to communicate meaning and enhance people's experience of the word. The one joke that I ever told in a sermon was about the man who prayed to be taken from "these low grounds of sorrow." That was until the angel of death came to answer his prayer.

Those who have heard me preach will likely wonder how I could be so seemingly stiff when my audiences laugh a great deal. The answer is that the humor is inherent in the gospel as presented. It attracts attention to and participation in the Word, not the preacher. If I portray Jonah as sad because these Ninevites didn't go to hell, how can anybody escape the humor? Given such involvement in serious substance, a laugh is one of the best indices of audience attention and participation.

• Can I use clichés or slang?

Some words have been used so widely, and for so many purposes, that they are drained of any real and present significance.

> I prefer to find fresh phrasings, otherwise our words slip through people's ears or, worse yet, they think they heard what we would never say. By finding new ways of stating our long-standing faith, we give people a chance to wake up and not just be bored.
>
> —Arthur P. Boers

Slang and colloquialisms sometimes fall into the same failure of significance as outworn language and clichés. But not always. They may actually serve as positive symbolic evidence of the preacher's willingness to be identified with the special speech community that uses the non-standard word. If this is the case, and the preacher is certain of the in-house meaning, then the slang may serve to diminish social distance.

I have found this especially true with youth. Language can be a means of bonding, no matter how much older the preacher may be. Using the idiom of youth, from time to time, can tell youth much about where the preacher's heart is. Even so, such words may need quick restatement in a parallel adult idiom so that all feel included.

CONCLUSION

What, then, may we conclude from this consideration of the polishing of sermons? Polishing can be a discipline we undertake with confidence and skill. It can be a joy and not a dreaded imposition. Polishing will be done well only if it is done with this attitude. As William Sloane Coffin says, "Get it written. Polishing then is fun."

The fear and dread of polishing is often born of a paradox of feelings. We want to say that our first flow of inspiration was just marvelous, thus needing no polish. It literally came from God. On the other hand, we are afraid to face the facts of our failures. We should rather fear going through our whole ministry without speaking personally, directly, and vitally with our people. Lifelong failure to speak in a way that does vital business with our people is a tragedy!
—Lowell Erdahl

Sermon polishing need not be feared, but it must not loom too large, either. It is possible to over emphasize the details of which we speak. It's not voice, vocal inflection, and eye contact that mediates the gospel. It's the kind of speech that loses itself in service to the moment, speech that draws attention to the idea, not to itself.
—Robin Meyers

Essentially, this sermonic work of art and engagement with people is a presentation to God, also directed to people.

Let the inspiration of the moment be a factor. The whole sermon process needs to be regarded as a joint venture with the Holy One, and every phrase of it needs to be open to the gift of inspiration.
—John R. Claypool

The gospel we preach needs all the human effort we can wisely offer to the service of the Lord. But, as we have already suggested, the goal is an *experiential encounter with God and the Word*. We preachers can go only so far in choreographing so awesome an engagement. When we have done our best, we can expect our Lord and Savior to say, "Well done." And when we have done less than our best, no matter how supposedly excellent that might be, we can anticipate that it will stand against us. The term *fear and trembling* applies to the tone of our efforts. Yet we also labor in joy, knowing that we will bring sheaves for the harvest. God accepts our best efforts with a graciousness beyond our fondest imagination.

BIBLIOGRAPHY

Callen, Barry L., ed. *Sharing Heaven's Music.* Nashville: Abingdon Press, 1995.

Craddock, Fred B. *Preaching.* Nashville: Abingdon Press, 1985.

Long, Thomas C. *Preaching and the Literary Forms of the Bible.* Philadelphia: Fortress Press, 1989.

Mitchell, Henry H. *Celebration and Experience in Preaching.* Nashville: Abingdon Press, 1990.

Severance, W. Murray, *Pronouncing Bible Names.* Nashville: Broadman and Holman, Publishers, 1994.

Wilson-Kastner, Patricia *Imagery for Preaching.* Minneapolis: Fortress Press, 1989.

7

WHAT TO DO WHILE PREACHING

Mitties McDonald de Champlain

Advising preachers on what to do in the pulpit is risky business. Opinions about pulpit behavior are as varied as the individuals who preach, and what we do or leave undone while preaching may influence significantly the effectiveness of a message. Because preaching is a speech act that happens through the agency of human beings, the sermon prepared in the study does not truly become a sermon until it is proclaimed in the gathered community. Delivering the message itself can be a terrifying prospect for many, beginners and pulpit veterans alike. When we also factor into the process that preaching is a very particular kind of public speech that is intended to be the word of God, it is no wonder that anxiety levels sometimes skyrocket. I'll never forget teaching my first preaching class years ago, where a student boldly confessed that she experienced existential isolation from her body every time she preached. Her remark is wonderfully reflective of the common fact that sermons are in many ways far easier to conceive than to deliver. Out-of-body experiences seem to be common for budding preachers. The moment of utterance is, in many ways, the moment of truth, since this is the time when all the hard conceptual labor spent on the sermon must be brought to life in a credible manner.

A central fact of the preaching life is that the sight and sound of the preacher are themselves carriers of meaning. The challenge, then, for every preacher is how and in what ways to become a fully embodied communicator when preaching. Sermons are offered as a means of enabling encounter with the divine. Thus preaching is an act of communion-making that requires the real presence of the person doing the proclaiming. How to *be* good news while preaching the good news is the concern of this chapter. In fleshing out the details of our subject in consultation with the preachers surveyed, I will consider those things in voice and body that may enhance or inhibit us when we preach, with a view to emphasizing the liberating fact that we have many options in discovering the available means of communicating the gospel aloud.

GOALS

• Be authentic.

Authenticity is the key term and the ultimate goal for communicating the gospel in our time. Effective communication is more a function of being *open, honest, relevant*, and *real* than it is a result of being *dynamic, powerful, forceful*, and *eloquent*. This is not to suggest that these two clusters of words are polar opposites when we consider delivery of sermons. I do want to affirm, however, that there is a hierarchy of value here. Matters of character have always been central to the understanding of what makes sermons work well. The great nineteenth-century preacher Phillips Brooks, in a classic and oft-repeated phrase, asserted that the truth of the gospel is mediated "through personality." Personality is communicated through nonverbal as well as verbal symbols. There is no escape from the reality that preaching is a self-offering. To ring true while preaching, then, preachers will want their manner and mannerisms to be true to themselves and true to life.

> I was somewhat puzzled by the question about what to do while preaching until I realized that my answer must be: *Be a preacher.* Let me explain.

We are all aware of the popular caricature of a preacher—the solemn character, wearing special clothes (whether official or not), speaking with a special voice, as if he or she had never enjoyed a night out and thoroughly disapproved of others doing so. Many young preachers are tempted to avoid any trace of this caricature and lean over backwards to earn the coveted compliment, "No one would ever think you are a preacher." Years of army service taught me that it's the chaplain who is not afraid to be a chaplain and doesn't strive to be one of the boys who is appreciated. So let the preacher be a preacher and not pretend to be otherwise.

—David H. C. Read

• Use a natural delivery.

There is nothing remarkable about this goal; it is sanctified common sense. Still, natural delivery is for me one of the grand essentials of communicating the gospel authentically and effectively. It means acknowledging that the only way we can be true to what we preach is by being who we are while preaching. While this may sound a bit like typically American, New Age thinking, I am always relieved to remember that this principle can be traced back to Archbishop Richard Whately in his 1928 handbook *Elements of Rhetoric*.

The practical rule to be adopted is . . . not only to pay no studied attention to the Voice [and body], but studiously to *withdraw* the thoughts from it and to dwell as intently as possible on the Sense [of material]; trusting to nature to suggest spontaneously the proper emphases and tones.

All our nonverbal response—everything we do while preaching—wants to be a result of an inner emotional and mental activity, not a substitute for it. Such a commitment keeps our delivery from becoming mechanical.

I believe that we preachers should engage in direct, personal, natural communication with our people and that this happens when we are thinking of and responding to our own thoughts as we share them. We are not thinking about our words or ourselves or anything else except the message we are seeking to get across to our listeners. Or, to put it another way, our thought should be on our message and our eyes on our listeners as we seek to bring the two together.

If we do not speak naturally when we preach, the problem may be homiletical or pathological or both! Have we been taught wrongly? Do we have bad habits of preparation and delivery? Do we have a distorted image of the preacher? Are we following the wrong models? Do we have deep inner anxieties and insecurities that keep us from being ourselves? If we don't speak naturally when we preach we need kind confrontation, at least some instruction, and perhaps some psychotherapy to set us free to dare to be ourselves.

—Lowell Erdahl

• Be appropriate.

Every congregation will have a set of expectations for what constitutes effective expression from their preacher. Preachers need to remember this when they preach. Almost every question we have about what to do while preaching can be answered by reflecting on whether or not the behavior fits the particularities of our text, our people, our context, and ourselves. For example, many of us carry deep within us a virtuoso performance model of preaching to which we think we need to conform if we are to be considered able at the preaching task. If preachers, however, try to model a style of delivery that doesn't suit them, then they may run into short-term and long-term difficulties in the credibility department.

Similarly, we may as individual preachers like to move out and away from the pulpit. But if the custom of the congregation being addressed is that the sermon is always preached from behind the pulpit, then the preacher needs to incorporate that expectation into his or her choices about what to do in delivery.

INSTRUCTIONS

A Conversational Quality of Voice

One of the key attributes of the effective preacher is the natural conversational character of his or her voice. Here preachers want to keep in mind that preaching is the act of sharing a natural public conversation with a congregation. And in discovering their own voice in the pulpit, preachers want to exhibit their natural rhythms, which is technically the sound flow of the voice made up of phrasing, pausing, inflection, and pace. Each person has a characteristic way that they speak in real life; vocal rhythm is the dynamic equivalent to a person's thumbprint. Partly what gives authority to the things we preach, what assures people that we are real, is that our voices reflect the full, natural sound of *us*. The sense of a message may be dramatically affected by the presence or absence of our own unique vocal rhythm. Whenever we hear feedback that a preacher sounded wooden, mechanical, or unreal, we are usually hearing that the preacher failed to recover their natural rhythm at the moment of utterance. Retaining the particularity of our natural voices is key.

> I want my voice to sound like it does every other day of the week, although I may enunciate more clearly and speak more loudly than I do on the telephone. I try to dissolve nervous ticks as they develop and may ask someone in the congregation to help me spot them. I allow silences in my delivery, especially at transitions, but never for the sake of drama alone. I use gestures a lot, especially when I am telling a story. I make a point of seeing what I am talking about in the air around me and touching it as I go.
> —Barbara Brown Taylor

Congruency in Communication

The effective preacher maintains a certain harmony or consistency between verbal and nonverbal expression. I like to tell preachers that they have *two* vocabularies—one verbal, the other nonverbal. Preachers understandably spend a great deal of time crafting the verbal sermon. Sometimes, however, they forget that how they sound out those words in tone and intensity, and how they punctuate those words with body language, may have a significant impact on the message received. For example, I have heard student preachers tell of bone-crushing defeats in their lives while smiling broadly. And we all have no doubt heard someone proclaim how much God loves us with a kind of intensity that for all practical purposes seems quite angry or hostile. The tone of voice and movement of the body want always to fit the particular words being preached.

> I believe the face of the preacher is particularly important. Sometimes anxiety freezes our faces. However, as we ourselves enter the message in preparation, we begin to feel the joy, sadness, assurance, uncertainty or whatever we want to share in the sermon.
>
> The word is congruence. Everything about the minister—face, voice, gestures—should be geared to communicate the message.
>
> —Charles Bugg

Empathy for the Material

Feeling deeply into material at the moment of utterance is the key to releasing the voice and body to speak the word. Spend enough time with the material prior to delivery to fully internalize it. A lively and vivid sense of material will enable the preacher to do this. Practicing out loud is not nearly as important as reviewing with concentrated and undivided attention what the words of the message are.

Delivery can't be separated from how we prepare a sermon or how we prepare ourselves for a sermon. Whether a minister uses a manuscript, outline, or nothing in the preaching event, she or he needs to internalize the message so that what is communicated is both known and felt. It's not enough to write a manuscript and to read the words correctly.

—Charles Bugg

Self-forgetfulness while Preaching

Exaggerated preoccupation with self and how we are doing while preaching is usually what produces unnatural, mechanical, awkward behavior. Unselfconsciousness at the moment of utterance, on the other hand, tends to produce far better nonverbal response. By directing attention away from self and focusing intensely on the message and congregation, our preaching will proceed with much greater ease and fluency.

Self-forgetfulness helps us to focus on the other. This can draw us into full communion with the people during preaching.

Think of the people: Sally, who just lost her husband; the Olsons, whose son was just diagnosed with severe manic depression. Forget yourself and think of the people. Pray, preach the Good News of a loving God who walks with them in their daily lives and daily relationships.

—April Larson

Choosing a Mode of Delivery

One of the central concerns for most of us who preach is what sort of material to take with us into the pulpit. Should we preach from full manuscript, outline, notes, or no notes at all? If we use no paper support, should we memorize or extemporize our remarks?

The basic answer to these questions is that preachers must select from the available options a mode of delivery that will best enable them to preach the good news in the least inhibited way.

> As for what sort of written material should be taken into the pulpit (manuscript, outline, note cards), the point is not that one is always superior to the other, but that all prompt the preacher to speak in the most *conversational* tone possible, and not consume so much energy in reading that there is nothing left over to give the presentation an extemporaneous quality.
>
> —Robin Meyers

No mode of delivery is entirely risk free. If we script, we may have to fight harder against losing our natural vocal rhythm. If we speak extemporaneously, we may risk not having the best words at any given moment to articulate our ideas. If we speak from memory, there is always the danger of having a memory lapse in trying to repeat word-for-word what we have prepared.

I personally prefer to work from a complete manuscript because it allows me a precision and economy of speech that the extemporaneous mode does not always guarantee. I also like the comfort and security provided by the script; it is a safety net. It liberates me to be totally involved with the people and the message. I speak the manuscript the same way that I talk, in my own natural voice.

Some preachers combine approaches.

> I preach with a manuscript, but I usually include in every sermon a narrative portion for which I have written down only a key phrase. That way I can maintain complete eye contact with the congregation for several minutes. I do not actually read my manuscript, but I keep it at hand for ready reference if I need it. By the time I am at the point of delivering a sermon, I know it. It is very much a part of my heart, a part of my spirit, and therefore I am not chained to my notes.
>
> —Joanna Adams

Other preachers find that working entirely note-free in the pulpit is more beneficial and freeing to them.

I have learned to preach without notes for two reasons. First, I find looking back and forth at a manuscript or notes throws off my sense of connectedness with the people present. I also like to look into people's eyes and incarnate the reality that I am here as an honest, caring human being who wants to make real connection with their lives and am not just reading a paper that may well be interesting truth, but of very little existential importance to that moment.

          —John R. Claypool

I personally do not like to read a sermon because I feel that I am keeping the Spirit from coming through. I think writing the sermon is an excellent preparatory exercise, but I would not take the written text with me to the pulpit. If I forget something that I thought was important, maybe it is only because God did not consider it as important as I did! I have to prepare with great care and diligence, but I must deliver it in the full freedom of the Spirit that I know is at work in me. I do my best to prepare, but in the final analysis, I am merely an instrument of the Spirit. After all, it is God's word that I try to proclaim and interpret and not my own! I am grateful to be used, but not so arrogant as to think that I have the last and final word.

          —Virgilio Elizondo

The Ready Position while Preaching

To enable the voice and body to function at full capacity, I have long advised my preaching students about the technical importance of being in a proper stance for communicating: comfortably erect, shoulders back, weight evenly distributed on both feet. Good posture is a better guarantee of optimal voice production and projection. Such physical readiness also frees the body for natural movement in response to the spoken word.

Nonverbal Vocabulary

It is possible, through practice, to expand and enhance all of the extraverbal cues that we use to embody the sermon—gesture, other kinesic movement, eye contact, facial expression, tone, and intensity. Similar to the verbal vocabulary, I believe that nonverbal vocabulary is something to be carefully thought through and developed.

Many of our preachers stress the need for eye contact with the congregation while preaching. While this may seem like a self-evident truth in contemporary American culture, there are both practical and theological reasons for maintaining visual engagement with the congregation.

> I always begin my sermon by first surveying the congregation, scanning the faces, and meeting the eye of many. This prevents me from the easy temptation of launching into my sermon and helps me connect with many people who are present.
>
> I maintain frequent eye contact throughout the sermon. This helps people listen and also helps me gauge where people are in relation to my words. Sometimes I realize that the sermon is not connecting, for whatever reason. Sometimes I see someone who feels challenged or another who feels excited. Sometimes I'm in the midst of a sermon and see someone who might be receiving the sermon differently than I intended. Sometimes I see someone whose life experience might cause him or her to disagree with me. In most such circumstances, I make a mental note to follow up with that person soon after our service.
>
> —Arthur P. Boers

> I want my listeners to know they are my partners—we're praying for the Spirit to fall upon us all, not just the preacher. I look around before saying a word. I want to see people in every corner, including a choir behind me and people in the balcony. I want to make a connection with these part-

ners before a word comes out of my mouth. This time also allow me to breathe, sense the Spirit's presence, and feel grounded in the space. It's very important to look at people and not read the sermon.

—Barbara Lundblad

Beyond eye contact, of course, there is a whole universe of discourse that can be created through gesture and other bodily movement. We typically say in communicative studies that a gesture is a movement of any part of the body to convey some thought or emotion, or to reinforce oral expression. The particular personality of each preacher determines his or her preference for movement. Our preachers demonstrate the rich variety of options the preacher has:

I move a lot when I preach; sometimes I move out of the pulpit into the center aisle. I don't plan gestures; they seem to come organically along with the words. But I know that's not true for everyone. If gestures don't flow naturally, I advise preachers to rest their hands lightly on the pulpit. Awkward gestures are distracting and worse than no gestures. Ask someone to give you feedback or watch a videotape of yourself. Ask: Do I always look to the right? Do I brush my hair out of my eyes (common for women with longer hair, but also for men)? Do I list to the left? Do I have a strange smile on my face for no reason?

—Barbara Lundblad

I seldom use my hands in preaching. I tried for a time and it always felt forced; parishioners urged me to be natural and not to worry about whether or not I use my hands. This means that on those occasions where I do use my hands, those movements have more of an impact.

—Arthur P. Boers

THINGS ENCOURAGED AND DISCOURAGED

Things Encouraged

• Project the voice.

Project loudly enough to be heard in the particular space in which the sermon is preached. In a sanctuary without electronic sound equipment, observe the following rule of thumb: speak loudly enough to be heard by a person in the last pew. If the worship space has proper sound equipment, stay positioned in such a way when speaking so that the full benefit of the sound system comes through. Listen carefully to judge when the voice is sufficiently filling the liturgical space.

• Control the breath.

If the Divine breath is going to flow through our preaching, then the practical importance of having enough physical breath to support our remarks cannot be overestimated. This requires deep breathing instead of shallow breathing. Always try to catch a deep breath during major pauses in the sermon and catch smaller breaths when there are natural breaks of phrase in the address. This should enable an almost constant column of air for utterance.

• Use natural pitch.

Be sensitive to pitch level while preaching. As a rule, the higher pitched our voices are, the more air we require in producing tone. The lower our voices are in pitch, the more we need to support our remarks from the diaphragm since we are releasing air more slowly. It is probably desirable to use one's normal speaking pitch, given our concern for naturalness and authenticity. There is no need to try to produce a lower or higher tone of voice than is natural and comfortable for the individual preacher.

• Prepare the sanctuary.

Allow for adequate time before the worship service begins to attend to any of the technical details that will affect the message. Ensure that the lessons upon which the sermon is based are properly marked in the Bible to be used. Confirm that the sound equipment is on, and determine whether there is a glass of water in the pulpit if required. Visiting preachers may also want to ascertain by phone in advance the size and shape of the pulpit. Sometimes the space available for a manuscript or notes is tiny, and manuscripts of traditional size cannot be easily and unobtrusively laid out. It is, in other words, essential to rule out technical problems in advance that might distract from the preaching event and overall worship service. The more planning in advance, the more likely our chances of ease and spontaneity in preaching.

• Remember prayer and contemplation.

Allow time for prayer and contemplation prior to the beginning of worship. Good preaching is both an artistic and a spiritual discipline. Every preacher will want to find a way of giving the self over to Christ before the proclamation begins. A line from a psalm, the Lord's Prayer, or "Lord have mercy" repeated silently may help. Use any practice that initiates the releasing of self into God's time and care.

Things Discouraged

• Do not imitate other preachers.

Do not try to mimic someone else's style of presentation. To be natural and credible, we must always aim to do those things while preaching that suit our own identity as preachers. As Dr. Samuel Johnson said, "Almost all absurdity of conduct arises from the imitation of those we cannot resemble."

• Avoid excessive nonverbal behavior.

It is not uncommon for beginning preachers to attempt choreographing movements and pauses. This, however, tends to look artificial and mechanical, creating extraneous nonverbal distraction instead of reinforcement for the sermon. Avoid nonverbal behavior that may interfere with or overwhelm the verbal content of the sermon. Sometimes, for example, we think that in order to be authoritative we have to speak using great intensity and dynamism in gesture from beginning to the end of a sermon. Instead, strive to engage the voice and body with a full sense of what is being said. Variation in rate, pitch, tone, and intensity are the natural outcomes of our vivid realization of the material being preached.

• Try not to get distracted.
Short of a crisis (verbal interruption, fire, heart attack), do not let the unexpected occurrence or other common disruptions during worship distract from the preaching task. Be prepared for all contingencies—from sirens outside the church to crying babies, coughing parishioners, and equipment failures inside. It takes a great deal of poise, concentration, and adaptability to hang in there when things go contrary to expectation. But all these sorts of possibilities need to be factored into our thought about what to do while preaching.

BEST ANSWERS TO QUESTIONS

• How do I eliminate performance anxiety?
Always remember that a certain amount of creative tension is essential for us to preach at our best. The corny and shopworn saying, "A preaching class will not help you get rid of the butterflies, but will help you to get them to fly in formation" is worth remembering. Preaching in many ways is like giving birth, and there is no escape from the natural birth pangs of anxiety that go along with the office of preaching itself. So our efforts should be aimed at developing a variety of coping mechanisms to help us deal with our fears.

Let the preacher expect to suffer, to agonize, to struggle while giving oral expression to what has been prepared. The sermon as delivered is not a recital, a memory lesson. Each word, phrase, sentence must issue from the preacher's lips as if discovered anew, afresh, experienced for the first time, coming alive for her or him in the eyes, nods, smiles, tears of the people

—Walter Burghardt

If we stay fully alive to the fact that preaching is an act of self-offering that celebrates the good news of God in Christ, we are more likely to be able to achieve a salutary level of self-forgetfulness in our encounter with the assembly.

Of course, there is also the matter of disabling nervousness. This must be minimized when we preach. One helpful way of coping with our nerves is to visualize in a concentrated way every facet of the worship service, including the sermon itself, before the service takes place (preferably the night before). Create a positive picture of what the whole occasion will look like. This can promote relaxation and confidence.

We can physically prepare ourselves for the act of preaching by drawing in several deep breaths to fill our lungs and then slowly releasing them. I usually try to do this during the hymn that is sung prior to the gospel lesson. It is quite soothing and can be done unobtrusively.

- How can I get rid of distracting habits like use of verbalized pauses such as "uh" and "uhm" and random shifting of weight from side to side?

If we have learned to do things in casual conversation that become distractions in public utterance, we first need to have these things brought to our attention. Video tape is a wonderful non-threatening way of having a good look at our behavior while preaching. Once we become mildly self-conscious about what requires adjusting, we can then practice *not* doing these things on occasions where we are *not* preaching, such as conversations or meetings. In these situations, we can afford to focus on the behavior itself. Practice changing mannerisms in safe environments in order to develop a capacity for eliminating the undesirable habit. The voice and body are really very adaptable if we work at conditioning our reflexes.

- How do I keep from looking down at my manuscript while preaching?

There is nothing wrong with looking at a manuscript as long as one does not constantly drop the head down to do so. This breaks our connection with the people. Retain full engagement with the congregation while preaching by simply glancing down with the eyes, not the head.

- How do I get rid of a monotone?

When I encounter people who have monotonic voices, I first look at the words of the sermon to be certain there is enough evocative language to invite some vocal variation. Sometimes sermon content has a flat affect, in which case the verbal style requires some imaginative adjustment.

Then the key is to think and feel deeply into the material to be preached. If we are fully attentive to the lively and glowing words on the page or in our minds, it will be naturally easier to reduce monotonous presentation.

CONCLUSION

The received wisdom of our preachers has provided ample and eloquent support for our overarching goal of authenticity in preaching. The good news of this chapter is that how an individual preaches a sermon depends entirely upon who she or he is. The options of what to do while preaching may be as particular and varied as the people doing the proclaiming. All our behavior communicates. It is up to each preacher to determine what is effective for any given occasion.

Perhaps it would be fair to say that the delivery of a sermon is the first place where we practice what we preach. This is the ritual action where we can, with God's help, become the incarnation of the gospel we are called to proclaim by word and example.

Authentic preaching, then, is a process of being obedient to and abandoned within our subject matter when we speak. Fred Craddock encapsulates very well the grand essentials of what to do.

> Once the sermon begins, the total self becomes servant of that message—the voice, the face, the hands, the mind, the emotions, the imagination. All one is and has is burned as fuel in the preaching. One is aware of everything and of nothing. The message is delivered by re-experiencing it in public, and when it is finished, one is both exhausted and exhilarated.

Thanks be to God!

BIBLIOGRAPHY

Bartow, Charles L., "Delivery of Sermons," in William H. Willimon and Richard Lischer, eds., *The Concise Encyclopedia of Preaching*. Louisville: Westminster/John Knox Press, 1995.

Marshall, Paul V.,"Delivery" in *Preaching for the Church Today*. New York: The Church Hymnal Corporation, 1990.

Rice, Charles L., *The Embodied Word: Preaching as Art and Liturgy*. Minneapolis: Fortress Press, 1991.

Pitt-Watson, Ian, *A Primer for Preachers*. Grand Rapids: Baker Book House, 1986.

8

COORDINATING WITH THE REST OF THE SERVICE

Thomas H. Troeger

Churchgoers attend services, not sermons. They go to worship, not to preaching. Clergy who focus all their energies preparing for the sermon without careful attention to the other elements of the liturgy will offer a distorted version of the Christian traditions of corporate prayer, and may obscure the efforts of the Holy Spirit to reach people through a wide variety of means other than the sermon.

Furthermore, our multimedia age is conditioning people to communicate in many different modes. A variety of liturgical expression is more able to engage our culture than one that is focused exclusively upon the sermon, as powerful as that means of communication remains.

> When we see the service as an integrated whole, even most die-hard Protestant services need not stand or fall on the basis of the sermon alone.
> —Arthur P. Boers

Such an integrated perspective not only leads us to give more attention to all the elements of the service. It also helps us to adopt the appropriate posture in our souls when we preach.

> The worship does not arrange itself around the sermon; the sermon is a part of the worship service. The sermon should be delivered as an act of worship.
> —Fred Craddock

There are important pastoral consequences when preachers center all their efforts on the sermon without adequate attention to its place in the total pattern of the liturgy.

> What people can grow to resent is the feeling that preachers have plugged their sermon into a service whose other components were of no real concern to them.
> —Robin Meyers

Thus for reasons of faithfulness to the traditions of Christian corporate prayer, effective communication, and pastoral sensitivity, it is vital that preachers clarify their principles and methods for planning and leading worship. In the material that follows we will see a variety of perspectives on this task, especially since the contributors represent a spectrum of liturgical traditions. But what is striking throughout the variations of their detailed suggestions is the similarity of intention: to glorify God, to provide order and integration while remaining open to the Spirit, and to keep the sermon in its proper perspective as a vital but not overcontrolling element of the entire service.

GOALS

There are two ways of defining the goals for worship. One is to speak of the goals of the particular service that we are immediately planning, and the other is to identify the larger historical and theological understanding that shapes all of our liturgical leadership. This second goal will be present whether we articulate it or not. And if we are not clear about it and pursue only the first goal, we may succumb to perpetuating worship that is sloppy or susceptible to any fad that comes along.

> Our aim should be to accept or devise a form of worship that is truly catholic in the deepest sense of that much misunderstood word, but be on our guard against it becoming an icon never subject to the slightest change.
>
> —David H. C. Read

The word *catholic* is not a denominational term but an ancient way of referring to the church universal. To keep in mind our place in the church universal is to stay connected to the wisdom of our ancestors and to a global view that lifts us beyond the constriction of considering only our own personal and local needs.

While all of us are members of the church universal, each of us participates in a distinctive community of faith. When we are planning and leading worship we need to know our tradition's history and spiritual character.

> I stand with a liturgical tradition, and this shapes the way in which I understand how the parts of the service, including the sermon, are to come together.
>
> —John Vannorsdall

The "I" here is not an isolated ego that can foist upon the congregation whatever it wants. There are boundaries and understandings that are historical and communal that the preacher and liturgist must honor.

In sum, our goal is to maintain our sense of being part of the church universal while honoring all that is best about the distinctive identity and practice of the tradition in which we stand. And it is this goal that orients our efforts as we turn to more detailed methods and principles for planning any particular sermon and service of worship.

INSTRUCTIONS

Because seminary training and theology are so heavily invested in verbal expression, it is easy for preachers to forget the importance of music, space, movement, and vision, yet all of these are vital dimensions of worship. As one plans worship it is important not simply to think in terms of words, but all the other things that will be done and seen. Ours is an incarnational faith. The Word did not become words. The Word became flesh, and so our liturgical planning needs to consider the many other ways that worship incarnates the gospel.

Music

Perhaps the most obvious way to expand our perspective beyond exclusively verbal liturgical expression is by working with our church musicians.

> Ministers have often failed to realize what a resource we have in a devoted organist and how much the gift of a well-coordinated service owes to his or her understanding and cooperation. What a joy it is to share in the worship of a church where there is an obvious and fruitful harmony between pulpit and organ loft, and how sad it is when this is missing.
>
> —David H. C. Read

Notice the way that Read puts the matter. He does not say that ministers need to become experts in music. Rather they need to appreciate and work with their musicians as a resource. Nowadays this will often include more than coordinating pulpit and organ loft. I think, for example, of excellent gospel rock musicians with whom I have worked. One group in particular was exemplary in the way they coordinated synthesizer, guitars, drums, and vocalists with the sermon, prayers, and response of the congregation. It was not music as entertainment, but music as prayer. The principle here is one that rises above differences of musical taste. No matter what the musical style the issue is the same: striving to fit music and language together in a way that is congruent with the design and flow of the whole service.

> I rely heavily on the minister of music to do much of the specific planning of worship. He and I discuss our philosophies of worship, what we are attempting to do, and I trust his judgment in the coordination and planning of the service.
> —Charles Bugg

This attention to musical resources can work primarily at two different levels. The more common one for most ministers is to focus upon the words of what is sung by the congregation or the choir.

> I tried hard to incorporate some words from both the hymns and anthems into my sermon. I did this in part because people tend not to think seriously about what they are singing.
> —William Sloane Coffin

Being attentive to the words of hymns and anthems, however, does not always mean that the preacher will choose texts that support the sermon. Sometimes there is an effort at deliberate juxtaposition.

> While it is helpful to select hymns that reinforce the theme of the sermon, I do not find it necessary. Sometimes it is better to let the hymns preach their own sermons, filling in gaps left by mine. For instance, on a Sunday when the sermon concerns the requirements of the law, I might shop for some hymns that celebrate God's grace.
> —Barbara Brown Taylor

Whether seeking support or contrast with the sermon, the principle is the same, namely, to consider carefully how the words that are sung will function in the overall design of the service.

It is important not to focus on words alone. Music has its own way of moving people, and if preachers cannot play or read music themselves, it is essential to try an unknown hymn out with a musician before selecting it. Hearing the musical quality of the piece may help decide where in the liturgy it can be used most effectively.

> I would also advise that hymns have a rhythm that coordinates with the flow of worship: upbeat processionals, meditation middle hymns, and songs of gratitude and praise to leave by.
>
> —Robin Meyers

Other Arts in Worship

I have started by considering music because it is the art form most employed by most traditions, and it is often the one that awakens the greatest depth of feeling. However, music, like the words of the sermon, depends upon hearing, and hearing is only one of our senses. Because of the historical biases of many traditions, hearing has been the privileged sense of worship, but it is important to note that many of our experienced preachers have come to see the inadequacy of stressing the auditory sense to the exclusion or diminution of others.

> Our Mennonite heritage and theology stressed simple sanctuaries. Nevertheless, our congregation has been invaluably gifted with creative and artistic people who are visually oriented. They work hard to arrange the sanctuary or displays in the sanctuary that contribute to the overall theme of the worship.
>
> —Arthur P. Boers

To use various arts as a means of communicating the gospel is not something that preachers and liturgists can do casually. It takes thorough planning just as an excellent sermon does, and it often involves the preacher's working with people who are skilled in areas of which the preacher has little knowledge. When this is done with care, then there are rich possibilities for worship.

> Consider the gift to the liturgy of worship of drama, dance, poetry, painting, and other expressions of the beauty of holiness *and* the holiness of beauty. Too often this is neglected or else is treated as something we can use in the service of gospel. We forget that the church has often been the forum for great literature, music, and other arts. We need more thought, as we seek to coordinate, about the role of the arts in the worship of the church.
> —David H. C. Read

Preachers and liturgists sometimes corrupt the use of an art by assuming that they must explain in words what art expresses through other means. Perhaps the most egregious example of this is the penchant for putting words on banners and other hangings instead of trusting that the Holy Spirit is bright enough to communicate through nonverbal means. This means taking the visual as a serious conveyer of Spirit and meaning.

> I personally do not like to use short messages on banners and much less on stoles or altar cloth. The Scriptures are full of very visual, poetic images that stimulate the imagination so as to experience freely the action and message of the Spirit. I find image coordination the most useful of all types of coordination.
> —Virgilio Elizondo

Once preachers and liturgists begin to think visually, any number of possibilities for enriching the service may present themselves, including new ways of engaging members of the congregation whose gifts might otherwise go untapped.

> Bulletin cover artwork can convey the central theme of text
> and sermon. Preprinted bulletins may already do this, but
> preachers can find drawings, enlist artists in the parish, or
> invite children to draw the cover once a month.
> —Barbara Lundblad

The deeper theological principle behind these instructions is the first and greatest commandment, which is to love God with all that we are. We use the arts not to make the service entertaining, but to engage the whole person in the act of worship. When this theological understanding feeds our efforts, then the use of the arts does not feel like a contrivance, but like a deepening of the gospel that springs from the heart of our worship.

THINGS ENCOURAGED AND DISCOURAGED

Things Encouraged

• Preach as an act of worship.
At the top of our preacher's list is not a method but a posture of the soul, a mode of being, a way of coming before God.

> The sermon should be delivered as an act of worship. Lis-
> teners can discern if the preacher is at home before God or
> is a speechmaker. The preacher can also help readers of
> Scripture do that as a significant act of worship.
> —Fred Craddock

• Train liturgical leaders.
Asking people to join in liturgical leadership does not automatically increase the sense of participation among the congregation. If lessons and prayers are mumbled or not presented with the requisite attitude of worship, it may decrease the sense of participation. People feel left out when they cannot see and hear.

In recent years the concept of being inclusive has become increasingly important to many worshipers. Unfortunately, inclusiveness has sometimes been narrowly applied only to language. As important as language is, there are also other dimensions to being inclusive: those who lead worship need to be visible and audible to the entire congregation, and they need to maintain the dignity and reverence which the community expects of someone in their liturgical role. In most cases, this means training participants who are going to lead the service. It is unwise to assume that because people can read, they will know how to read in a large public space, or because people are prayerful in their personal life, they will know how to lead a prayer in a service. Instead, allow adequate time for planning, training, and rehearsing. This does not turn the service into a show, but rather makes the act of worship a more effective vessel for the Holy Spirit.

All of this requires a substantial and regular investment of time.

> I advise monthly meetings with the worship committee and weekly meetings with other participants in the service.
> —Fred Craddock

And even those regular meetings will not always be adequate in themselves, since the process of planning and preparing often turns up ideas and glitches that were not initially foreseen.

> Frequently, we [musician, liturgists, children's story teller] consult each other along the way.
> —Arthur P. Boers

Once again there is a deeper principle at work behind the specific suggestions, namely, that faithful worship grows out of a careful process of prayer and planning. Preachers and liturgists give themselves to the strenuous work of preparation out of love for God and a desire to help the community when it gathers to express its praise and to renew its faith.

• Respect traditions, cultures, and contexts.
Preachers and liturgists strive to honor the intention and customs
of the particular tradition in which they work, realizing that others bring different understandings to the task. The essential ingre-
dient is respect for the distinctive character of a community.

Culture and tradition, for instance, influence such practicalities
as how long a service ought to be. Writing for a culture that is
highly conscious of the clock, Charles Bugg observes:

> We try never to exceed an hour in the service. My feeling is
> that in most of our traditions we experience diminishing
> returns when the service runs more than an hour.

Traditions with a different sense of time would find this advice
restrictive and possibly unfaithful to their understanding of following the Spirit. The important principle is that preachers and
liturgists honor the understanding of time that is part of the community in which they work. Since this can vary from congregation
to congregation within the same denomination, it is wise when
starting a new pastorate or visiting in an unfamiliar church to
inquire about how long the sermon and service are expected to
last. These may seem small matters to one who is first setting out
as a preacher and liturgist, but in fact they are significant because
they help to define how a community orders its corporate life.

Things Discouraged

• Don't over-plan.
As in most of life, every affirmation carries with it a qualification.
Thus, the importance of planning and coordinating can be carried
to an extreme so that there is no allowance for the uncontrollable
and unexpected movements of the Spirit.

> I know that liturgists are very much into coordinating the
> worship service. I think this tends to cut down on the joy and
> spontaneity of the assembly and often leads to choosing
> music that is neither too good nor well known. Some plan-

ning and coordination is certainly necessary, as for any fiesta, but I think that plenty of space should be left for the action of the Spirit.

—Virgilio Elizondo

Differences about planning and spontaneity represent different cultures and theologies. No one liturgical formula fits all traditions.

I respect other traditions that find no necessity to coordinate the elements of the service and depend upon the Holy Spirit to provide the congruities, which so often does happen. I do think that the Holy Spirit probably has a better chance when those responsible have done some homework.

—John Vannorsdall

There is, then, a need to balance order and freedom, to allow room for both careful preparation and the inexplicable movement of the sovereign Spirit of God.

There are two extremes to avoid in dealing with the matter of coordinating the different elements of a service. One is the extreme of giving little or no thought at all to the question. Likewise the prayers, except possibly the prayer and hymn immediately after the sermon. Thus the mood of the service may be totally foreign to the main emphasis of what is heard from the pulpit. The other extreme is represented by the preacher who makes a fetish of coordination and eliminates any possibility of the spontaneous. Many may be left feeling that they have been hearing or watching a performance according to the book rather than sharing in a drama whose end will be a new experience of a community surprised by joy or by some other gift of the Holy Spirit, the Giver of life.

—David H. C. Read

• Avoid self-satisfying tinkering with worship.

> Changes in forms of worship are not to satisfy a preacher's passion for tinkering with liturgy and to satisfy his or her own dreams and prejudices.
> —David H. C. Read

This does not mean that liturgical change is never desirable or possible. Let preachers find in their role a constant encouragement to act as leaders who have a responsibility to the community, to honor its tradition while opening people to the fresh winds of the Spirit.

BEST ANSWERS
TO QUESTIONS

• What is the nature of the relationship between preacher, liturgist, and congregation in worship?

Our answer to this question will determine the impact of our leadership upon the congregation. If we think of the service as our turf, if we feel threatened by the contributions of others, if we fail to work in a gracious and professional manner with the musicians and others, then we can stack words of faith from the floor to the rafters in our sermons, and they will not make a bit of difference to anyone because our liturgical leadership will convey a completely different message—one of fear, egotism, and control. This is what people in communication studies refer to as a meta message, the signal that our entire way of being and acting communicates.

Thus, several of our preachers describe the relationship of preacher, liturgist, and congregation by drawing upon a famous metaphor from Søren Kierkegaard.

> It is important to remember that Christian worship is intended to be highly participatory and not just a spectator event. God is the true audience for all that is done in worship. The

worshiper is the actor who does the significant work of confession and thanksgiving and learning and resolving. The
clergy and the choirs are the enablers, the prompters, those
who make the whole process flow.

—John R. Claypool

The metaphor is not merely intriguing. It has practical consequences for the way we present ourselves and the attitude that we
convey and encourage in the congregation. At all times, we need
to remember our goal is not to impress others with the excellence
of our performance but to help the whole congregation take part in
the worship of God.

> If the preacher speaks as though God were the primary
> audience and the congregation secondary, all other partici-
> pants and the congregation will likely respond with a
> heightened sense of worship.
>
> —Fred Craddock

• Should the entire service be thematic?
There are different schools of thought about this, varying not
only with the perspective of individual preachers, but also
reflecting different liturgical traditions and cultures. However,
even those who tend to favor a thematic approach offer some
important qualifications.

> I do not try to force everything into a rigid mold. The fact is
> that people come to a service with different needs. For
> example, the Hymn of Praise may touch on the theme of
> the sermon, but I do not expect to sing a hymn that simply
> reflects everything that will be said in the sermon.
>
> —Charles Bugg

Do not let the sermon overcontrol all your choices. The range
of human need and the spectrum of prayer—from glad and joyful
thanksgiving to lament—are simply too great to be constricted to
the themes of one sermon.

As a rule, I would advise against coordinating the whole service around one theme. People come to church with many
pressing personal concerns and can feel left out of a service
whose focus is quite different from theirs. Prayers of thanksgiving and intercession need to be inclusive.

—William Sloane Coffin

One thing that drives people toward thematic services is their
understandable desire to provide a coherent experience of worship,
something that does not seem to the congregation haphazard, as
though it were simply a collection of assorted spiritual fragments.
However, it is important to remember that most liturgies, especially those that have been shaped over the centuries, have their
own inner coherence, a connectedness that is rooted in the deeper
levels of the One whom we worship.

Word and sacrament, word and worship, are intimately
related, that the sermon serves as the bond between the
liturgy and that of the bread and cup, that the word must
mediate between the fixed forms of the liturgy and the spirit and freedom of a particular people.

—Walter Burghardt

Several of our preachers, representing a range of denominations
and traditions, affirm that the liturgy possesses its own unique
coherence.

The gospel has enough natural cohesiveness, and the great
themes of the life of faith are so interconnected that they
often weave their own magic without our help.

—Robin Meyers

All in all, I am content with a worship service that contains a
variety of expressions. The focus on God in Christ in Scripture and sacrament is usually enough glue to hold any service together.

—Barbara Brown Taylor

• What is the best way to develop prayers for corporate worship? Leading a congregation in prayer is different from offering prayer in the solitude of our own souls. Although the practice of personal prayer is essential to anyone who is going to be an effective liturgist, there are other factors and understandings involved in the act of corporate prayer. For one thing, prayer in most traditions refers to far more than only those parts of the service that are designated by the word. The entire service, everything that is done and said, is a form of prayer. Thus standing, bowing, clasping hands, singing, moving, being silent, and all the other actions of the service come together as one act of corporate prayer.

When preachers and liturgists turn to consider the formulation of specific spoken prayers within the context of the entire service, it is helpful to remember that there is no need to reinvent the words and ways of prayer. Tradition, as well as the Bible, is a rich and virtually endless resource. Christians have been offering corporate prayer for two-thousand years, and they have left us a legacy of forms and types of prayer that we can either use word for word or adapt to the peculiar needs of our congregation. In drawing upon these traditions we provide people with a helpful sense of the past, reminding them that we are not the first to undergo the common lot of humanity. Our ancestors, like us, knew pain, grief, and loss and they have left a heritage of words and ways of praying that can open us to the presence of the same compassionate God in whom they found refuge.

> Those who pray can also learn the differences in kinds of prayer: pastoral, invocational, confessional, eucharistic, and benedictory so that all the prayers do not sound the same, differing only in length.
> —Fred Craddock

To draw upon the variety of prayers is a way of simultaneously keeping a church in touch with the tradition of the church universal and the span of human need that is present whenever a congregation gathers.

• What is the best way to handle conflicting desires for contemporary and traditional worship?

A good place to begin is to find out what people have in mind when they use the words *contemporary* and *traditional*. These terms often mean amazingly different things to different people depending on their upbringing and church experience. Preachers and liturgists ought never to assume that their definition is another's. Furthermore, a dictionary definition will not suffice. People need to fill out the definition by giving examples of music and ritual actions that give a precise picture of what is in their heads.

It is essential to have a worship committee consisting of the worship leaders, including the chief musician and a sampling of the congregation, so that those in favor of contemporary and traditional services are both represented. There is no one recipe for solving these conflicts, but it is essential that preachers and liturgists encourage by word and behavior a respect for all parties as they work out how the church will address the conflict.

> Our people often have strong differences of opinion and feeling concerning traditional versus contemporary and formal versus informal worship. They are unlikely to be receptive to either our preaching or our leadership if they feel excluded from the worship planning process.
> —Lowell Erdahl

There is wisdom here. Instead of coming down in a rigid stance, Erdahl articulates a process of inclusion. If preachers and liturgists are faithful and sensitive in leading the group through this process, then it often becomes a source of reconciliation, of living the gospel in community.

> My experience is that most congregations respond when changes in forms of worship are carefully explained as they are introduced. The purpose of having a well-coordinated service should be made clear. It is to fulfill the biblical injunction to worship God in Spirit and in Truth.
> —David H. C. Read

CONCLUSION

When preachers and liturgists consider the breadth and variety of issues raised by our experienced preachers, it may seem that preparing and leading worship is strenuous work that demands a lot of time and energy. That is in fact the truth of the matter. But it is worth all of the effort. For one thing, it means that the sermon no longer has to bear the full weight of the service. Or course, the sermon makes its own demands in preparation and delivery. But preachers who realize the capacity of the whole service to be a vessel of the Holy Spirit will find a greater freedom in the act of homiletical creativity. No longer burdened by thinking they must meet every need through their words, preachers can attain a finer degree of focus and liberation in their homiletical efforts.

Preachers who honor the importance of ritual embody in their liturgical leadership a more wholesome way of being faithful, one that encourages the congregation to bring all that they are to God. And when this happens, then preachers, liturgists, and congregation members all together have a sense that

> No hour in the week approaches this one in quality or importance.
>
> —Fred Craddock

BIBLIOGRAPHY

Costen, Melva Wilson, *African American Christian Worship*. Nashville: Abingdon Press, 1993.

Davies, J. G., editor, *The New Westminster Dictionary of Worship*. Philadelphia: Westminster Press, 1986.

Doran, Carol and Troeger, Thomas H., *Trouble at the Table: Gathering the Tribes for Worship*. Nashville: Abingdon Press, 1992.

Procter-Smith, Marjorie, *In Her Own Rite: Constructing Feminist Liturgical Tradition*. Nashville: Abingdon Press, 1990.

Willimon, William H., *Worship as Pastoral Care*. Nashville: Abingdon Press, 1979.

9

FEEDBACK

Craig A. Loscalzo

If beauty is in the eye of the beholder, good preaching is in the ear of the hearer. What one person describes as good preaching, another person may call a lot of things, but preaching would not be one of them. If a person considers the preaching of a tent revivalist good preaching, they might consider preaching within a liturgical church as nothing more than a boring lecture. At the same time, a person from a liturgical setting may think that the preaching of a tent evangelist constitutes nothing more than ranting and raving. Personal experience dating back many years often frames the judgment of what characterizes a good sermon.

My own approach to preaching bears out this reality. I preach sermons laden in narrative tone and content. Along with a multitude of preachers, Eugene Lowry's *The Homiletical Plot* and Fred Craddock's work on inductive preaching have influenced my approach to sermon development. However, some churches where I have had the opportunity to preach as an itinerant or interim preacher were used to propositional preaching packed with deductive sermon forms. When I would greet people leaving the sanctuary, they would say things like, "That was a good *talk*" or "I liked your *stories*." They could not say, "I liked the *sermon*" because for them what they heard was not a sermon; it did not fit their definition of what a sermon must be in terms of form and feel.

If sermons are so subjectively judged, how in the world can we ever get helpful and authentic feedback about our preaching? How do we gain and process sermon feedback? Is negative feedback helpful or harmful? How do we use feedback as openings for pastoral care or ministries of social action? Such questions frame the heart of this chapter. But not all preachers think feedback is necessary or helpful.

In a preaching practicum where peer evaluation made up the bulk of the course, a student once told me that he could not evaluate the preaching of a fellow student. He said, "If God gave the sermon to him, what right do I have criticizing it?" I wish I had responded by saying, "Well, God doesn't have to worry about getting a grade in this course, but you do!" I tempered my words by saying, "Whether you like it or not, people will always be evaluating your preaching—in casual conversations, around the dinner table after church, and in Sunday school classes. You may be surprised by how much you can learn from the feedback of others."

The following comments about feedback will help to frame our discussion:

> I have often likened preaching without feedback to driving golf balls in the dark. Unless we hear from our hearers, we will never know if we are hitting the green or going off into the woods.
>
> —Lowell Erdahl

> Preachers have to develop a feedback indicator that is fairly accurate. People seem to be programmed to give standard feedback such as: "You did a good job today, Reverend;" "I really enjoyed your message today;" or "Mary needed to hear that message, but she wasn't here today." Feedback of this magnitude is not to be taken lightly. A better gauge, however, is when people take the time to call a day or two later to express gratitude for the sermon or when people go into details and share how the message was helpful and useful to them. The lack of feedback cannot be allowed to hinder the preacher; therefore, it is crucial for the composer and deliverer of the word of God to

determine when he or she has satisfactorily done what they were called to do.

—James Henry Harris

One week, for some reason, I found myself genuinely struggling with the gospel text for the following Sunday—John 3:1-17. I worked hard, probably twenty to twenty-five hours on the sermon, and when I delivered it, I was still not sure that I found the most helpful way to express the great, deep mystery of God's love for the world. After worship, a usually reticent parishioner said "Hello," shook my hand, started to walk away, and then turned back and said quietly, "Joanna, I do not know what to say about what you said today except that I'm grateful to God that I was here to hear it."

We can never know whether or not our preaching has been successful in the sense of being useful to the purposes of God. It is for us only to do our best and to remember that the Spirit of God is like the wind, blowing where it will.

—Joanna Adams

Good sermon feedback helps us in the process of doing our best in the awesome task of preaching. In this chapter, we consider ways for getting and processing sermon feedback.

GOALS

• To improve our preaching.
The primary goal of feedback is better preaching. Feedback should always be a means to that end and not an end in itself.

• To develop informal and formal feedback channels.
Feedback comes in more-or-less two primary forms: Informal feedback, which comes to us casually and must be more-or-less looked for and caught in order for it to be helpful. Formal feed-

back, in which the preacher intentionally seeks out specific types of responses.

Informal feedback. Preachers would be helped by remembering that the sermon conversation began long before the specific sermon was preached and, in the best of circumstances, will continue long after the actual sermon ends.

> As to sermon feedback, I have but two suggestions: First, if one is approachable and accessible, there will be feedback. At first it will not be profound or critical; the listener will have to test the preacher to see if feedback is welcomed and heard. Increasingly, feedback will be thoughtful and often full of memories, both painful and joyful. A sermon may thus evoke thoughts and feelings more associated with another time and place, and perhaps even another preacher, than with the present sermon. Response to such feedback may be immediate or may call for more extended conversation. Since feedback involves memory of not one but many sermons, the preacher should not be too elated or too depressed by any comments from listeners. Secondly, since the sermon grows out of and contributes to the congregational (and sometimes public) conversation, I suggest introducing into conversation with persons present or absent at its delivery portions of the sermon. This keeps the sermon alive and at work; it also removes the awkwardness some people feel about initiating response to the sermon with the one who preached it.
> —Fred Craddock

> The most important type of feedback is over the course of time as I hear testimonies of how people have been changed because of the sermons. One self-proclaimed atheist who regularly followed my sermons told me, "I still don't believe in God, but thanks to your sermons, I have discovered what it means to be a true and authentic human being."
> —Virgilio Elizondo

I always regard the sermon as the first word in an ongoing conversation, not the last word on anything. Those who serve as resident pastors have the opportunity of unceasing dialogue with their people through all personal and pastoral interactions.

—John R. Claypool

It's true, of course, that when a parishioner gives feedback (positive or negative), more is being said than is actually said. It may be a signal that pastoral care is needed. It may be a signal that there are deep political differences, which can make objective listening all but impossible. Or it may be a signal that the sermon was just lousy!

If you are lucky enough to have close friends in the church who can be honest, without worrying about harming the relationship, then pay attention to their comments. And most of all, pay attention to your spouse. There is no better critic, and no more honest consumer of your sermons.

—Robin Meyers

Another aspect of informal feedback is the immediate feedback that happens in the very moments of preaching and after worship.

Probably the best feedback for sermons is what one gets while preaching! To a considerable extent you can tell what is happening unless your eyes are glued to notes or manuscripts.

—J. Philip Wogaman

I get a great deal of feedback during the preaching of a sermon. I am acutely aware of the congregation's eye contact with me, their stillness or restlessness, their silence or coughing—even their breathing. While this does not give me specific information about how my sermon is being heard, it does tell me whether or not I am being listened to.

—Barbara Brown Taylor

I know when I am making sense to them by their reactions. By their looks they tell me if they are with me or if I have lost them.

—Virgilio Elizondo

Informal feedback also occurs immediately after the sermon is preached.

After each sermon, I go to the back door where I receive informal feedback. I try to listen carefully to what was heard and how it seemed to be interpreted. During the week people will comment on different parts of the sermon. It's important for me to hear not only what they heard but also to recall the form in which I delivered it. For example, was it a story and what was the story about?

—Charles Bugg

I am always very available at the end of the service at the back of the worship space, and have made it a point to never be rushed here, but to stay at the church as long as there is anyone who has something that they want to share. I listen with keen attentiveness to the things that people say about the sermon as they leave. Many times a person will ask me, "I heard what you said this morning, but what about this or that?" Their question will often lead me to the next word in our ongoing pastoral conversation. I work in the southern region of the United States, which means that people have been conditioned to not be totally frank in their face-to-face encounters.

—John R. Claypool

I often receive feedback at the door, although this is generally the positive variety. If the sermon raises questions or doubts, I will usually receive a telephone call on Monday asking for an appointment. I take this as a high compliment, even if the response turns out to be negative.

—Barbara Brown Taylor

Please keep in mind that these types of informal feedback are subjective in nature. One person's scowl of anger may be another person's way of showing intense interest or engagement. The only way to know how to interpret a hearer's look would be to ask the hearer what he or she was thinking. But noticing what's happening during the sermon and listening astutely to comments after the sermon can only help the preacher become more effective.

Another informal way to get feedback is to listen to the sermons of others.

> I like to listen to the sermons of others and ask myself, "What touched me, what moved me, what challenged me in their sermons?" Through the sermons of others, I critique my own sermons. They are a type of indirect feedback.
> Virgilio Elizondo

Formal feedback. Formal feedback takes more work than informal feedback because it is an intentional attempt to gain an understanding of how our congregations hear us as we preach. Obviously, direct feedback will be less subjective than indirect feedback, however, all feedback resides in the realm of subjectivity. Remember one person's measure of a good sermon is not another person's measure.

> From time to time I ask specific questions of my listeners. I preach to one women's group twice each week, at an informal service on Thursday and again at a principal service on Sunday. I have asked them to pay attention to the differences between the sermons (the first delivered from the altar rail without notes, the second from the pulpit with full manuscript) and to tell me about the differences in their hearing.
>
> Many preachers make good use of an official sermon feedback group. Sunday is not the best day for this, however. It seems easier to give and receive responses to a sermon after it has had time to cool off.
> —Barbara Brown Taylor

I have found it helpful to arrange for a few people to join me for coffee in a room separate from the usual after-service social hour. I thank them for their willingness to help me improve as a preacher and then ask a question appropriate to the sermon. For example, "What were you imagining when I described Jesus riding down our Palm Sunday street?" It doesn't take long to discover what elements of the sermon were not heard at all and which ones were understood, or were understood in ways I had not intended. The emotional response to the sermon is usually apparent in the context of such a discussion. If we think we have to do this every Sunday, we'll probably not start. Why not do it for a season and then let it rest?

—John Vannorsdall

Charles Bugg reminds us that formal listening groups should not become an ongoing burden for participants.

I have not used official listening committees for several reasons. I'm certain that my own fear has something to do with it. However, beyond that I want to be careful that I do not create a group of people who are listening so critically to the sermon that they do not have the freedom to experience worship. If ministers use an official group to give feedback, they probably need to change the members of the group about every three months.

INSTRUCTIONS

Separating Ego from the Process

Preachers remain fully human. We all like to be liked. It becomes extremely difficult to separate ourselves from our sermons. Criticizing a sermon has been likened to saying something about a mother's firstborn child. If we have poured heart and soul into a sermon's composition, it becomes hard to determine where the sermon ends and we begin or vice versa.

> I would advise preachers that in processing feedback, the most important thing to do is separate one's ego from the process. On the whole, preachers are compulsive pleasers who will receive a hundred compliments at the door and then get an ulcer over a single criticism.
>
> Learn to criticize your own sermons. You will find that preaching is so much a function of personal growth that your early efforts would be almost embarrassing now. So forgive those people who had to listen to them and set your own high standards. Most of all, don't forget what you are called to do.
>
> —Robin Meyers

Positive and Negative Feedback

Listen and evaluate both positive and negative criticism. Every preacher would wish that every sermon he or she preached would be nominated for the Best Sermons Hall of Fame. Remember, however, that even those who made it to the Baseball Hall of Fame struck out, a lot! We learn from what we do well; we learn from our mistakes and shortcomings. Listening and evaluating what hearers liked and did not like about our sermons will always make us better preachers in the long run.

> Experience has also taught me that it is worth trying to make sure that if the feedback is specifically asked, it should not be from your fans but your critics!
>
> —David H. C. Read

> Really listen to even the most negative criticism. Behind the most hostile comment is an element of truth.
>
> —April Larson

My best advice would be not to take the praise too seriously and not to be too unhinged by negative feedback. A good preacher will receive a certain amount of both. One of the things one learns is that the same sermon is bound to hit different people in different ways. Sometimes I am surprised by extremely positive feedback to a sermon I thought was mediocre at best, and then the reverse can occur when I thought I was delivering one of the greatest sermons of my ministry and the response was a dull thud! But if we do our work well, it will be helpful to some. And we can learn from our mistakes as well as our successes

I think it is important not to give too much weight to feedback from a handful of extremely vocal people. We can learn from that, but often such people do not really represent the congregation as a whole.

—J. Philip Wogaman

I would also advise the preacher to remember that negative feedback hides itself, while positive feedback doesn't. Just because you don't hear back on something doesn't mean that there is universal rejoicing.

—Robin Meyers

A Variety of Models

Find the ways and models that work best for you and your situation. Be willing to change feedback methods as the circumstances dictate. The following are ways five of our preachers have gotten and processed formal feedback. Listen to their advice, analyze your preaching setting and situation, and determine how you can best implement some of their suggestions.

I've found that a structured time and intentionality are the most helpful.
• A weekly text study group within the congregation (we met on Wednesdays); the first part of the session can be a reflection on last Sunday's sermon. If a preacher is open to

genuine questions and disagreements, as well as compliments, the group will begin to be more honest and helpful.

• Structured sermon discussion during coffee hour after worship once a month.

• Ask two or three people to be reflectors each week; one of them might read the gospel text aloud to the preacher on Monday so the preacher hears the text. It may be helpful to give these reflectors three questions or open-ended statements, such as, "I got lost when . . ." or "When the sermon was over I was thinking. . . ." Try to vary the reflectors: retired people, teenagers, single people, married people, men, women, newcomers, and old-timers.

• Tape sermons and listen alone or with a colleague.

• Trade sermons with a friend or mentor (trade tapes if there's no manuscript), ask for specific feedback: Did this image work? Where were transitions unclear?

• Participate regularly in preaching workshops that include feedback on sermons.

—Barbara Lundblad

I have practiced and commend two forms of feedback. One is to invite written comments from our listeners and the other is to invite a small group of kind and honest people to meet with us for a discussion of preaching. I think it is helpful to have feedback cards in the pew racks every Sunday that can be headed "Sermon Reactions" or "Preaching Suggestions," followed by a statement such as "To help make preaching a two-way street, please write your sermon reactions (positive and negative) and suggestions on this card and return it with the offering or hand to an usher. You need not sign your name. Thank you." A larger card or bulletin insert might be titled "Partnership in Preaching" and begun with this paragraph: "You are invited to be a partner in the preaching process. Please share your sermon reactions and suggestions on this form. Return in the offering plate, hand to an usher, or mail to the church office. You need not sign your name." This is then followed by these three questions with space for comments: (1) "What did you appreciate in this sermon?" (2) "What detracted?" (3) "Suggestions for better preaching?"

When selecting people to meet with us for discussion of preaching, I believe the choice should be the preacher's and that we should pick people who are both kind and honest. It is scary to invite feedback. Someone has said that, "When we open our mouths, we let people look into our hearts and minds," and that's a scary business, but I believe it is worth the risk. I still remember the comments of a hardware dealer from my first parish who told me in one of these groups that I didn't look at them when they sat in the front pew and that I often spoke at such a rapid, steady pace that, "It's easy after a while to sit back and let it go over your head." I needed those comments and have tried to respond to them by paying special attention to the people down front and by daring to pause and break the steady pace of my preaching.

I encourage preachers to meet with such a group five or six times a year. During the first session, I had them tell about the kind of preaching they had experienced. During the second, I asked them to tell me everything positive they could think of concerning my preaching. Then beginning with session three, I invited them to share things that distracted and their suggestions for improvement. I laid down the rule that while positive comments could be general, all negative comments had to be specific and concrete. I pointed out that while a general positive comment such as, "Thanks for a good sermon" is helpful encouragement, a negative comments such as, "I didn't like your sermon" is worse than useless. If there is something about our preaching that someone doesn't like, we need to know exactly what it is so that we deal with and hopefully correct it.

—Lowell Erdahl

I advise every preacher:

• To have a small group of parishioners (men and women) meet with him or her a week before the sermon to read the liturgical lessons aloud, meditate on them, and express thoughts that have occurred to them on the meaning of the readings and their pertinence to the realities of life within the community.

• To have a small group of parishioners prepared to submit their reactions to the sermon, either individually or (preferably) as a group—and this a day or so later. The postservice comments ("Nice message, Reverend" or "Thanks a lot, Father"), while appreciated, are hardly helpful.

• To have audio tapes—better still, video tapes—made of at least one sermon a month, so as to experience what the congregation sees, hears, even suffers.

I suggest:

• That preachers occasionally have copies of a sermon ready for distribution after the service. I believe David Read did this for years at Madison Avenue Presbyterian Church in New York City. Such a policy would put helpful pressures on a preacher's preparation, invite listeners to ponder the sermon more fruitfully afterwards, and allow for further feedback.

—Walter Burghardt

The easiest way is to ask for reactions. After certain sermons, particularly those on controversial issues, it's well to schedule a talk-back right after the service. If the opposition doesn't show up, theirs is the blame. The chances are good that they're sullen but not mutinous.

If people say your sermons are too long, too dull, too anything, I wouldn't hesitate to go to someone for help. Maybe a little help would go a long way.

—William Sloane Coffin

I have on many occasions intentionally structured a feedback process that frees people to be more honest by giving them the cloak of anonymity. For example, I have handed out simple questionnaires in the church bulletin that ask salient questions like: "What was the central thrust of the sermon today? Was it easily understood, or were there terms and images that were obscure? What did you find yourself feeling and thinking and wondering as you participated in this word event?"

In encouraging people to give honest feedback, I am often able to measure exactly how effective my preaching style is. On other occasions, I have asked several people whose judgment I trust to commit to six weeks of response to the sermon. I provide them a room and a tape recorder and allow them to meet after the service and talk freely about their impressions of what has just happened. This is more taxing on people's honesty, because I do listen to the tape and I do know who these folk are. It is so important that the preacher be a perennial learner, which of course is what Jesus' image of a disciple actually is. Once again, if I am essentially a gift-giver in my preaching, and not a reputation earner, I can hear negative impressions and sift out what really is valid and can improve my preaching.

—John R. Claypool

THINGS ENCOURAGED AND DISCOURAGED

Things Encouraged

- Become an astute observer, seeking intentional opportunities to gain formal and informal feedback.
- Listen to all feedback—negative and positive—constructively.
- Analyze your own preaching through the use of audio and video tapes.

- Take time to listen to, read, and analyze the sermons of other preachers. This will help you hear the feedback of others productively.
- If you agree with certain criticisms, work on correcting only one at a time. In other words, build one good habit before correcting the next problem.

Things Discouraged

- Avoid listening to just a few people within the congregation. The broader the range of feedback, the better.
- Avoid listening to only your fans or only your detractors.
- Avoid taking negative criticism personally.
- Do not avoid feedback.

BEST ANSWERS
TO QUESTIONS

- The topic of feedback seems to include the idea of a preacher's openness or vulnerability. How open should a preacher be in soliciting feedback?

Visitors have often expressed surprise to me at hearing a preacher expose himself to critical questions in public discussion and questioning within ten minutes of the benediction. I find that one of the best times and places for this kind of feedback is immediately after the service if thought has been given to milieu, acoustics, and other such practical matters.

- Does a congregation have a responsibility to help improve the preaching they hear, or is good preaching only the responsibility of the preacher?

  It's up to the minister to indicate to the members of the congregation that good preaching is in part their responsibility.

They have to allow him or her adequate time for preparation, and then provide the nurture which comes with
thoughtful affirmation and appropriate suggestions.
                                                    —John Vannorsdall

• Do I have to implement change in response to every negative
  criticism I hear?

Before responding to any criticism, ask yourself, based on the best
preaching theory that you know, have read about, and understand:
Is the criticism a valid criticism in terms of preaching? If you
answer "No," perhaps you can help the one giving the advice to
see your perspective as a trained preacher. If you answer "Yes,"
then ask, Is the criticism valid in my preaching circumstance? The
answer to the second question will then have to be handled in
light of how much you are able to tolerate change in your approach
to preaching. At least you have analytically looked at the feedback
and have made an intentional decision about it.

CONCLUSION

Preaching, like all communication, is improved through the effective use of feedback. Good preachers not only listen to feedback
but actively seek and process it in formal and informal ways. Cultivate a listening ear to those who hear you preach, and maybe
because you have listened to them, they will hear you.

10

ESSENTIAL RESOURCES FOR PREACHING

Thomas E. Ridenhour

Edmund A. Steimle defined preaching as the sensitive inter-twining of three stories: the congregation's story, the preacher's story, and God's story (the biblical story). Throughout this chapter I will use these three categories to organize resources that are essential for preaching. Choosing the essential resources for preaching clearly depends upon the ecclesial and theological tradition in which the preacher stands. These decisions are also influenced by the preacher's understanding of the purpose and intent of preaching and the nature of the good news conveyed by Scripture.

GOALS

• Collect a mixture of familiar and challenging resources.
Although our choices for resources will be shaped by our own traditions and perspectives, they should also include resources that challenge us.

> It is important to include a diversity of viewpoints: Western European, Latin American, Asian, women, men, Jewish writers.
> —Barbara Lundblad

Be sure to read out of your theological and ecclesiastical tradition, so that you will not begin to view the world through denominational lenses.

—Robin Meyers

Various journals and periodicals are good. I subscribe to conservative evangelical and liberal mainstream periodicals—all usually challenge and have something to offer.

—Arthur P. Boers

• Organize resources in a comfortable place for study.

The preacher's library should be a comfortable place where thoughts are disciplined and the imagination sparked. Fred Craddock, who has helped me very much in my preaching and teaching over the years, concisely summarizes what is needed.

At the desk where the hard work of study is done, within easy reach should be a concordance, a Bible dictionary, a regular dictionary, and a Bible atlas. Some things can be called up, but some must be looked up. These basic volumes are not servants of the sermon unless they are immediately available. Around this desk are the commentaries gradually accumulated that have become trusted friends and the volumes of theological reflections on the major themes and issues of the faith. Not so near at hand but in the room are the books that treat pastoral, practical, and current issues of church and ministry. Near another chair, more comfortable, and beside a reading lamp are the journals regularly read as well as the novels, collections of short stories, and volumes of poetry to which one returns again and again. This room is shaped and furnished for the preacher who studies and reads and writes here. Church committees with a passion for color-coordinated decorating may help make the room presentable, but should understand whose place it is and for what purposes it is used. Parishioners need to know at what hours the preacher is at work here and respect those hours, barring emergencies.

—Fred Craddock

• Nurture our own humanity, faith, and ministry.

The preacher and the preacher's story are significant parts of the preaching task. Preachers easily find themselves caught up in the rat race of the regularity with which Sunday rolls around. We forget to care for ourselves as a major resource in our preaching. Do we take the time and energy to allow the word of God to address us in our own lives? Are we developing skills that will help us listen to the congregation and the community in which we live? Are we sharpening our own sensitivity to the world? Do we seek personal opportunities for growth that will stretch our minds and hearts?

> Continuing education is as important as the volumes in the minister's library. I recommend that courses at a seminary be alternated with courses taken at a local college, especially in the areas of creative writing, ethics, and sociology. Another degree is not important. What is in the preacher's library is probably not as important as what comes into his or her purview from day to day throughout the year.
> —John Vannorsdall

> I believe life is the essential resource for my preaching, and I do my level best to pay attention to it.
> —Barbara Brown Taylor

> None of us can read everything, but all of us can be continually reading something, including things that are not specifically theological. My wife, Carol, and I have been members of a book discussion group for over twenty years and, although all of the members are clergy and clergy spouses, we never read anything that is specifically theological. We meet once a month during the school year and usually read a novel or other book of common interest. All of us have confessed that if it had not been for that group we would never had read most of these books.
> —Lowell Erdahl

The attention that we as preachers give to the world and our own lives is not done essentially so that we can find or discover sermon illustrations or topics. The time and energy spent attending to our lives is primarily for the sake of deepening our own humanity and relationship with God. Anything we can do to strengthen and nurture our lives crafts our story as an essential resource for preaching. The more aware we are of the world around us and the people around us, the greater the possibilities exist that life will permeate and shine through our sermons.

INSTRUCTIONS

Resources for Exegeting the Congregation's Story

As the minister makes pastoral visits to homes, hospitals, or workplaces, sensitive listening provides good informal clues and insights into the real lives of churchgoers. What are they faced with each day? What do they worry about or celebrate? Have a journal or notebook handy to jot down important aspects of the congregation's story.

Beyond informal study of the congregation, it is important to formally study the congregation in both its present reality and historical existence. The minister can learn about the history of a congregation by reading minutes of congregational meetings, congregational histories, and doing oral history with members of the congregation. The community of faith did not arrive at its present situation overnight, even if it is a newer congregation. How is this congregation structured? Who are its members? Where does the actual power reside in the congregation? Do ongoing exegesis and interpretation of the congregation. Some resources that are helpful for guiding and structuring this exegesis are:

Jackson W. Carroll, *As One With Authority: Reflective Leadership in Ministry* (Westminster/John Knox Press, 1991).

Edwin H. Friedman, *Generation to Generation* (Guilford Press, 1985).

James F. Hopewell, *Congregation: Stories and Structures* (Fortress Press, 1987).

Roy M. Oswald, *Power Analysis of a Congregation* (Alban Institute, 1981).

Jackson W. Carroll, Carl S. Dudley, William McKinney, eds. *Handbook for Congregational Studies* (Abingdon Press, 1989).

Leonora Tubbs Tisdale, *Preaching as Local Theology and Folk Art* (Fortress Press, 1997).

The current denominational scene in our country reflects large numbers of congregations in conflict for a variety of reasons. Resources for understanding congregations in conflict include:

David W. Augsburger, *Conflict Mediation Across Cultures* (Westminster/John Knox Press, 1993).

David W. Augsburger, *Anger and Assertiveness in Pastoral Care* (Fortress Press, 1979).

William Easum, *Dancing with Dinosaurs: Ministry in a Hostile and Hurting World* (Abingdon Press, 1993).

Hugh F. Halverstadt, *Managing Church Conflict* (Westminster/John Knox Press, 1991).

Anthony J. Gittins, *Gifts and Strangers: Meeting the Challenge of Inculturation* (Paulist Press, 1989).

Mike Moore, *Reconciliation: A Study of Biblical Families in Conflict* (College Press Publications, 1994).

Ecclesiastical and denominational literature helps the preacher understand the congregation in the larger church context. Be sure to subscribe to denominational newspapers or newsletters. Denominational worship, polity, and program resources should always be close at hand. *The Christian Century, Christianity Today*, and Martin Marty's *Context* place the congregation's story in the context of the ecclesiastical world in which we live today.

News sources help to locate the congregation in the community and world. Reading the local newspaper, of course, is a must. Beyond the local scene, keep in touch with the world at large and new cultural trends by purchasing a weekly Sunday newspaper such as the *New York Times, Washington Post,* or *Los Angeles Times*. Subscribing to a weekly news magazine such as

Time, Newsweek, or *U.S. News and World Report* is also a good idea.

Depending upon the social location and demographics of the congregation, the preacher's library should include books on African-American culture, blue collar America, country music, gospel music, the men's movement, urban ministry, suburban ministry, New Age spirituality, and so on. This section of the preacher's library should also include resources that will help the preacher understand people in general. Purchase resources on human development and aging, domestic violence and child abuse, illness, suffering and pain, death and dying, racism and sexism, and family-systems theory.

Notice what people in the congregation are reading, watching on television, or listening to on the radio. Don't forget to observe popular culture.

> Pay attention to the books people are buying—not just to be with it, but to be able to converse in the idioms of the day. Read bumper stickers. They are the one-liners of our culture. Read letters to the editor and obituaries (the language of remembrance is often richly dishonest). And remember, commercials are the most widely consumed American art form. Our national motto might well be, "You can't be too rich or too thin."
>
> —Robin Meyers

> I recommend an occasional mystery story of high literary quality (P. D. James, for example), music that inspires—from Palestrina to Mozart to Amy Grant to the Grateful Dead to Red Hot Chili Peppers.
>
> —Walter Burghardt

Resources for Exegeting the Preacher's Story

As I have already suggested, our own faith relationship with God is crucial for us as preachers. How is our life of faith fed, nourished, strengthened? Where and how does God come to us to rattle our cages, to apply the balm of Gilead to our wounds, to forgive and free us, and to enlighten and sustain us in the complex world of ministry into which God has called us? How, in the community of believers, do we experience the presence and power of the Holy Spirit at work in our lives? Where, when, and how do we pray, sing praise, offer lamentations and intercessions for others and ourselves? Reflecting on all of these concerns helps us discern and live our stories as preachers.

In my opinion, many spiritual self-help books are sentimental and can turn honest self-reflection into narcissism. It is usually more helpful to think in realistic ways about our own lives and autobiographies. How do we tell our stories to other human beings so they're not sugar-coated, but realistic and honest? Reading the works of Frederick Buechner has been a great help to many in this regard. Buechner demonstrates the power of autobiography—honest autobiography. Reading autobiographies and journaling our own autobiography can help us to be realistic and humble about our own lives. We discover that we are not always the hero. Sometimes we are the clown or the dummy. Always, we are the one standing in the need of God's grace, mercy and forgiveness.

> I read anything by people such as Frederick Buechner and Annie Dillard—people like this make me think more deeply about life.
>
> —Charles Bugg

Regional novels—about life in the South, the Northeast, the Midwest, and so on—can help us to relate self-reflection to regional identity.

It is necessary to reflect from time to time on our theological presuppositions and worldview. Every preacher needs to keep up with his or her operative theology. When we are aware of this theology, we can be more intentional and comprehensive in our communication. Why is it that I am called and compelled to proclaim this message? Is that really God's good news for today, or just my own pet interest? Two helpful resources for discerning our own theological world view are:

James Hopewell, *Congregation: Stories and Structures* (Fortress Press, 1987).

W. Paul Jones, *Theological Worlds: Understanding the Alternative Rhythms of Christian Beliefs* (Abingdon Press, 1990).

Resources for Exegeting God's Story

Many resources contribute to the narration of God's story as it is revealed in Holy Scripture and has been formulated in the theological tradition of the church catholic. The Bible is the beginning point in this story. If the preacher knows the biblical languages (Hebrew, Greek, and Aramaic) then a copy of the Bible in those languages should be close at hand. Nearby should be a good lexicon and perhaps a Hebrew and Greek grammar.

• Standard Greek and Hebrew lexicons:

F. S. Brown, S. R. Driver, and C. A. Briggs, *A Hebrew and English Lexicon of the Old Testament, corrected edition* (Oxford University Press, 1952). Reissued as *The New Brown, Driver, and Briggs . . . Numerically Coded to Strong's Exhaustive Concordance* (Baker Book House, 1981).

W. Bauer, *A Greek-English Lexicon of the New Testament and Other Early Christian Literature* (tr. and ed. W. F. Arndt and F. W. Gingrich, rev. F. W. Danker; 2nd edition, University of Chicago Press, 1979).

• Standard Greek and Hebrew reference grammars:

E. Kautzsch (ed.) *Gesenius' Hebrew Grammar* (Clarendon Press, 1910).

F. Blass and E. Debrunner, (trans. F. W. Funk's) *A Greek Grammar of the New Testament and Other Early Christian Writings* (University of Chicago Press, 1961).

• Translations.

Regardless of the preacher's facility with biblical languages, the bookshelf should include at least three or four good English translations. I suggest:

New Revised Standard Version Bible (Oxford University Press, 1993).

Revised English Bible with Apocrypha (Cambridge University Press, 1989).

New Jerusalem Bible (Doubleday and Company, Inc., 1985).

Good News Bible (Thomas Nelson Inc., 1993).

Some will want to have a *King James Version* as well.

> Translations are very culturally conditioned and sometimes I have to get behind the cultural conditioning to discern the original intention and meaning of the text. It is quite interesting, for example, to see the differences between the *King James Version, The Jerusalem Bible,* the *Biblia Latinoamericana,* and the *Ecumenical Bible of France.*
> —Virgilio Elizondo

Reading the text in three or four different translations helps the preacher determine words or textual nuances that may need further study. These items can be checked out in dictionaries, word books, and commentaries. Certainly the preacher should make use of the translation that the congregation will hear read in worship when the sermon is to be preached.

• Concordances, wordbooks, and gospel parallels.

A concordance to the whole Bible should sit on the bookshelf next to these translations. Any one of the following concordances will do:

John R. Kohlenberger III, *The NRSV Concordance: Including the Apocryphal Deuterocanonical Books* (Zondervan Publishing House, 1991).

Edward W. Goodrick and John R. Kohlenberger III, *NIV Exhaustive Concordance* (Zondervan Publishing House, 1990).

James Strong, *Strong's New Exhaustive Concordance,* (World Publishing, 1992).

John Kohlenberger III, Edward W. Goodrick, and James Swanson, *The Exhaustive Concordance to the Greek New Testament* (Zondervan Publishing House, 1995).

I have found it helpful to have a concordance that lists with each English word the Hebrew or Greek word or words that are translated by the English word. This makes it easier to establish a quick reference to the word in Gerhard Kittel and Gerhard Frederich's multi-volume *Theological Dictionary of the New Testament* trans. Geoffrey Bromiley (William B. Eerdmans Publishing Company, 1971). Kittel and Frederich's dictionary is also available in a one-volume, abridged edition (William B. Eerdmans Publishing Co., 1975).

• Other helpful dictionaries for word study.
G. Johannes Botterweck and Helmer Ringgren, *Theological Dictionary of the Old Testament* 7 vols. (William B. Eerdmans Publishing Co., 1978).
Horst Balz (ed. Gerhard Schneider), *Exegetical Dictionary of the New Testament* 3 vols. (William B. Eerdmans Publishing Co., 1990). R. Laird Harris, Gleason L. Archer (ed. Bruce K. Waltke), *Theological Word Book of the Old Testament* 2 vols. (Moody Press, 1980).

• To compare texts between the four gospels purchase a copy of:
Robert W. Funk's *New Gospel Parallels, Revised Edition* (Polebridge Press, 1990).

• Bible dictionaries and atlases.
On the bookshelf next to translations and theological wordbooks should sit a good general Bible dictionary. The *Anchor Bible Dictionary* 6 vols., (Doubleday and Co., Inc., 1992) is unsurpassed among contemporary English language reference tools, although many still find much useful material in the old, somewhat dated, *The Interpreter's Dictionary of the Bible* 5 vols. (Abingdon, 1976).
Other adequate dictionaries are:

The *Mercer Dictionary of the Bible* (Mercer University Press, 1990).

Harper's Bible Dictionary (HarperSanFrancisco, 1985).

Holman Student Bible Dictionary (Holman Bible Publishers, 1993).

Tyndale's New Bible Companion (Tyndale House, 1997).

• For geographical questions, a Bible atlas should be available. I recommend either of the following:

Herbert G. May (ed.), *Oxford Bible Atlas* Revised by J. Day (Oxford University Press, 3rd ed., 1985).

J. J. Bimson, J. P. Kane, J. H. Paterson, D. J. Wiseman, and D. R. Wood, *New Bible Atlas* (InterVarsity Press, 1994).

• Commentaries.

What commentaries should the preacher use? These decisions should be influenced, in part, by the preacher's theological perspective and tradition. Include a variety of commentaries that represent the influence of different theological perspectives and traditions. Look also for commentaries by authors who use diverse types of biblical criticism: source, tradition-historical, form, redaction, social scientific, canonical, rhetorical, structuralist, narrative, reader response, poststructuralist, and feminist. To discover authors who best represent these critical approaches, look at the bibliography of books that summarize these forms of criticism, for instance:

Gordon D. Fee, *New Testament Exegesis: A Handbook for Students and Pastors, Revised Edition* (Westminster/John Knox Press, 1993).

Christopher Tuckett, *Reading the New Testament: Methods of Interpretation* (Fortress Press, 1987).

Steven L. McKenzie and Stephen R. Haynes (eds.) *To Each Its Own Meaning: An Introduction to Biblical Criticism and their Application* (Westminster/John Knox Press, 1993).

John H. Hayes and Carl R. Holladay, *Biblical Exegesis: A Beginner's Handbook* (Westminster/John Knox Press, 1983).

Daniel J. Harrington, S.J. *Interpreting the New Testament: A Practical Guide* (Michael Glazier, Inc., 1979).

Many of our preachers found it helpful to have a solid one volume commentary of the whole Bible in their library. Any of these three will do:
Harper's Bible Commentary (HarperSanFrancisco, 1988).
Mercer Commentary on the Bible (Mercer University Press, 1994).
The New Jerome Biblical Commentary (Prentice Hall, 1989).

It's a good idea to have as a goal several commentaries on each book of the Bible.

> I try to have two or three good commentaries on each book of the Bible.
>
> —Charles Bugg

Be careful about purchasing a whole series of commentaries. There are always some volumes that are not as helpful or consistent as others in the series. Be sure to look for authors whose theological perspectives are supportive or challenging. In my opinion, *The Interpretation Series* (Westminster/John Knox Press) is fairly consistent and well-designed for preaching and teaching in the church. I also recommend:
The Old Testament Library (Westminster/John Knox Press).
The Continental Commentary series (Fortress Press).
The New Interpreters Bible (Abingdon Press).
The Augsburg Commentary on the New Testament (Augsburg Books).
The Anchor Bible series (Doubleday and Company, Inc.).
The New International Greek Commentary series (William B. Eerdmans Publishing Company).
The Women's Bible Commentary (Westminster/John Knox Press).

Lectionary preachers should be certain to have commentaries on books of the Bible that appear most frequently in the lectionary.

Each year, when the lectionary calendar begins, it is a good idea to purchase a relevant commentary or two.

There are several relatively inexpensive series of preaching commentaries based on The Revised Common Lectionary. These books generally provide an interpretation of the lectionary texts and some homiletical and liturgical suggestions. They can be evocative and useful, but are only intended to be used near the end of the preacher's exegetical work, during the movement from text to sermon.

Three good ones are:

The Proclamation series (Fortress Press).

Texts for Preaching 3 vols. (Westminster/John Knox Press).

Preaching the Revised Common Lectionary 12 vols. (Abingdon Press).

The journal *Lectionary Homiletics* comes out monthly and is also a good lectionary resource. For the Hispanic American preacher, Virgilio Elizondo recommends Father Juan Alfaro's bilingual sermon notes published by the Mexican American Cultural Center in San Antonio, Texas.

• Theology.

Although the biblical tradition is the primary locus of the word of God for preaching, preachers also need resources that unfold the long history of the church's wrestling with and thinking about God's story narrated in Scripture. Be sure to have books by the giants in the history of the church: Augustine, Aquinas, Julian of Norwich, Hildegard of Bingen, Luther, Calvin, Wesley and others. Also include contemporary theological resources. Some of those mentioned by our preachers include: Karl Barth, Paul Tillich, James Cone, Rosemary Radford Ruether, Katie Canon, Jürgen Moltmann, Hans Küng, Letty Russell, Wolfhart Pannenberg, Jacquelyn Grant, Thomas Oden, Douglas John Hall, Marjorie Suchocki, Gabriel Fackre, Carl Braaten, Robert Jenson, Elizabeth Johnson, and Sallie McFague. Preachers should have several theologians who reflect the theological tradition of their denomination and other theologians who provide various counterpoints.

The preacher's library should also include books on theological ethics from a variety of perspectives.

> The preacher needs to focus on biblical ethics and particularly the ethics of Jesus.
>
> —James Henry Harris

Two excellent collections of readings in Christian ethics are:

Wayne G. Boulton, Thomas D. Kennedy and Allen Verhey, *From Christ to the World: Introductory Readings in Christian Ethics* (William B. Eerdmans Publishing Company, 1994).

J. Philip Wogaman and Douglas M. Strong, *Readings in Christian Ethics: A Historical Sourcebook* (Westminster/John Knox Press, 1996).

In addition to these collections, the preacher's library should include works in feminists ethics, African-American ethics, and bioethics. Another good resource is the *Westminster Dictionary of Christian Ethics* (Westminster/John Knox Press, 1986). Be sure to include a variety of perspectives on issues such as abortion, euthanasia, economic justice, genetics, the environment, human sexuality, and peacemaking.

• History.

> I find historical materials especially important and I grieve over the neglect of Christian history by so many preachers. Congregations are generally interested in the experience of Christians of other ages even when that means negative experiences we have to correct in our own time (such as the role of women in church and ministry).
>
> —J. Philip Wogaman

Several good historical sources are:

Williston Walker, *A History of the Christian Church* (one volume) (Macmillan, fourth edition, 1985).

Justo L. González, *The Story of Christianity* 2 vols. (HarperSanFrancisco, 1984).

Classics in Western Spirituality Series (Paulist Press, 1978).

Sydney E. Ahlstrom, *A Religious History of the American People* (Yale, 1972).

Mark A. Noll, *A History of Christianity in the United States and Canada* (William B. Eerdmans Publishing Company, 1992).

Rosemary Radford Ruether, *Women-Church: Theology and Practice of Feminist Liturgical Communities* (Harper and Row, 1985).

Carter Lindberg, *The European Reformations* (Blackwell, 1996).

James Livingston, *Modern Christian Thought: From the Enlightenment to Vatican II* (Macmillan, 1971).

Paul Bradshaw, *Early Christian Worship* (SPCK, 1996).

Theodor Klauser, *A Short History of the Western Liturgy* (Oxford, 2nd edition, 1979).

Cheslyn Jones, Geoffrey Wainwright, Edward Yarnold, S.J., and Paul Bradshaw (eds.) *The Study of Liturgy, Revised Edition,* (Oxford University Press, 1992).

Two dictionaries also provide brief historical essays and bibliographies that may be helpful for the preacher:

The Oxford Dictionary of the Christian Church (Oxford University Press, 1974).

The Westminster Dictionary of Theological Terms (Westminster/John Knox Press, 1996).

• Homiletics.

Every preacher's library should include several fundamental resources on the theory and practice of preaching. Excellent basic texts include:

Thomas G. Long, *The Witness of Preaching* (Westminster/John Knox Press, 1989).

Fred B. Craddock, *Preaching* (Abingdon, seventh edition, 1988).

Paul Scott Wilson, *The Practice of Preaching* (Abingdon Press, 1995).

Other rich resources are the works of David Buttrick, Tom Troeger, and others, including any of the contributors to the present work. For smaller articles and bibliographies relevant to the practice of preaching, consult *The Concise Encyclopedia of Preaching* (Westminster/John Knox Press, 1995).

Two excellent journals will help the preacher keep up with new developments in homiletics. The semi-annual journal *Homiletic* contains good reviews of books and items recently published that are of interest to every preacher. *Homiletic* also includes a list of upcoming preaching conferences for continuing education. *The Journal for Preachers* is also an excellent resource.

• Theological and biblical journals.

> I have found that theological journals put out by seminaries, like *Theology Today* from Princeton Theological Seminary, are exceedingly valuable. They often reflect what is coming in theological circles and keep one alert to the cutting edge of contemporary thought.
> —John R. Claypool

In the same way, I find *Interpretation* to be a good resource. Walter Burghardt recommends, and I would concur, that preachers take a biblical journal by subscription. He recommends the *Journal of Biblical Literature* or *Catholic Biblical Quarterly*. Depending upon the financial resources available, I encourage taking several journals that provide broad and diverse perspectives on issues biblical and theological.

• General reference tools.
For sermon editing and polishing, the preacher needs a good dictionary of the English language or the primary language being used for preaching. Many of our preachers say that an unabridged dictionary is crucial. Several said that preachers should own *Bartlett's Familiar Quotations* (Little, Brown and Company, 1992). A good, general encyclopedia is also nice to have around.

• Other resources of interest.

The range and diversity of books recommended by our preachers demonstrates some of the different kinds of interests or concerns that might be found in the preacher's library. Here is a list of other journals and books recommended by our preachers:

Journals

> *Sojourners*
> *Word and World*
> *Dialog*
> *Parabola*
> *The Living Pulpit*
> *Christianity Today*
> *Christian Ministry*
> *The Living Pulpit*

Books

Walter Brueggemann, *Finally Comes the Poet* (Fortress Press, 1989).

Christine M. Smith, *Preaching as Weeping, Confession and Resistance* (Westminster/John Knox Press, 1992).

Ronald Allen, *Contemporary Biblical Interpretation in Preaching* (Judson Press, 1984).

Annie Dillard, *Pilgrim at Tinker Creek* (HarperCollins Publishers, 1988).

Kathleen Norris, *Dakota: A Spiritual Geography* (Ticknor and Fields, 1993).

Audre Lorde, *Sister Outsider* (The Crossing Press, 1984) and *Burst of Light* (Firebrand Books, 1988).

Carter Heyward, *Our Passion for Justice* (The Pilgrim Press, 1984).

Cornel West, *Race Matters* (Beacon Press, 1993).

Anne Lamott, *Bird by Bird: Instructions on Writing and Life* (Pantheon Books, 1994).

Mary Oliver, *A Poetry Handbook* (Harcourt Brace and Company, 1994).

John Wain (ed.), *The Oxford Anthology of English Poetry* 2 vols. (Oxford University Press, 1991).

F. O. Matthiessen (ed.), *Oxford Book of American Verse* (Oxford University Press, 1950).

Philip Larkin (ed.), *The Oxford Book of Twentieth Century English Verse* (Oxford University Press, 1973).

Margaret Drabble (ed.), *The Oxford Companion to English Literature* (Oxford University Press, 5th ed., 1985).

The Bible Workbench (published by the Educational Center in Saint Louis).

Clarence Jordan, *Cotton Patch Version of Matthew and John* (New Win Publishing, Inc., 1970).

Ernesto Cardenal, trans. Donald D. Walsh, *The Gospel in Solentiname* 4 vols.(Books on Demand, 1976).

THINGS ENCOURAGED AND DISCOURAGED

Things Encouraged

- Be broad in building resources.
- Spend money for solid, stimulating, evocative resources.
- Be a good, sensitive listener to the congregation and the world.
- Initially purchase only those resources that are not readily available in a public library or a seminary or college library nearby.
- Continually build resources for preaching.

Things Discouraged

- Do not be narrow in resourcing.
- Do not be cheap in planning a budget for building a resource base.

BEST ANSWERS
TO QUESTIONS

• When do I have enough resources?
The smart mouth answer may be "Never!" yet the way life and the world changes so rapidly for us, there is some truth to that response. We need to be challenged, questioned, and stimulated constantly in our thinking and imagination. Our preaching will grow stale if we fail to do this.

• How do I know what are the best resources?
Trust your own judgment. Ask people you trust what they would recommend. Read journals that have bibliographies and book reviews. Take time to read and learn about authors to learn what their perspectives and interests are.

• How do I know when a resource is no longer current or relevant?
The publication date on some materials may be a clue to their continuing usefulness. How much is the resource related to the world in which you and your congregation now live? There are some timeless resources that have stood the test, but avoid using resources that contain interpretations and understandings that are outdated and irrelevant. Again, your own wisdom and the advice of people you trust can help you critique a resource.

CONCLUSION

After listening to our preacher's advice about resources, it is clear that individual perspective, tradition, and theological stance should shape the resources that preachers have in their libraries.

They also make it clear that the preacher should be broadly resourced so that a narrow perspective does not become a coffin in which one's preaching is slowly buried.

Preachers must be aware from the beginning that building a good library takes planning and careful budgeting. After a general accounting of the current prices of the basic texts suggested in this chapter the price tag came to nearly $6,000.00.

Careful attention to resourcing, however, pays high dividends in the pulpit:

• Biblical exegesis and theological interpretation will keep pace with biblical and theological scholarship.
• Awareness of self, congregation, culture, and world will expand and deepen.
• The homiletical imagination will stay fresh and energized.
• Knowledge of homiletical methods and options for practice will remain current and vital to the contemporary church.

All of these things are essential to a fruitful preaching ministry.

BIBLIOGRAPHY

Gordon D. Fee, *New Testament Exegesis: A Handbook for Students and Pastors, Revised Edition* (Westminster/John Knox Press, 1993).

Richard F. Ward, "Resources for Preaching," in William H. Willimon and Richard Lischer (ed.) *The Concise Encyclopedia of Preaching* (Westminster/John Knox Press, 1995).

Donald McKim, *The Bible in Theology and Preaching*, Revised Edition (Nashville: Abingdon Press, 1993).

George Kehm, "Scripture and Tradition," in P. C. Hodgson and R. H. King, *Christian Theology: An Introduction to Its Tradition and Tasks* (Philadelphia: Fortress Press, 1982).